IN THE WOODS
AND FIELDS
OF CONCORD

Edited and with an introduction by
WALTER HARDING

Selections from the
Journal of
Henry David Thoreau

SELECTIONS FROM THE JOURNALS OF

HENRY DAVID THOREAU

IN THE WOODS AND FIELDS OF CONCORD

Edited and with an introduction by
WALTER HARDING

Drawings by MADS STAGE

→P

A Peregrine Smith Book / Gibbs M. Smith Inc.
Salt Lake City, Utah 1982

Library of Congress Cataloging in Publication Data

Thoreau, Henry David, 1817-1862.
In the woods and fields of Concord.

Selected essays from the author's Journal.
1. Thoreau, Henry David, 1817-1862—Diaries.
2. Authors, American—19th century—Biography.
3. Natural history—Massachusetts—Concord.
I. Harding, Walter Roy, 1917-   . II. Title.
PS3053.A2   1982b   818'.303   82-10563
ISBN 0-87905-090-X

Introduction copyright © 1982 Gibbs M. Smith, Inc.

This is a Peregrine Smith Book
First edition
Manufactured in the United States of America.

Book design by Scott Knudsen.

Drawings courtesy Mads Stage.

TABLE OF CONTENTS

I*NTRODUCTION*

In the fall of 1837, Henry David Thoreau began to keep a daily journal. He had recently returned to his native Concord, Massachusetts after graduating from Harvard College; and Ralph Waldo Emerson, his friend and mentor, had urged him to begin such a record. Emerson himself had long kept a journal and, finding it a veritable storehouse for his lectures and essays, recommended the practice to Thoreau, whose writing he wished to encourage.

Born in Concord on July 12, 1817, the only one of the famous Concord writers who was actually a native of the town, Thoreau from childhood on spent a good part of his time wandering the fields and woods, rivers and ponds of Concord. Although only eighteen miles from the metropolis of Boston, Concord, with its population of only two thousand, was essentially a rural community and one could slip into the countryside within a few minutes from any back door. When Thoreau returned to Concord from college, he almost immediately established a routine of spending from two to five hours each day usually in the afternoon exploring the countryside,

observing the constantly changing phenomena of
nature. His parents, particularly his mother, had
fostered his interest in the outdoors from childhood,
regularly taking the children on walks and picnics.
It was said that so great was her delight in nature

that one of the Thoreau children was nearly born on a family nature walk. Thoreau's older brother John kept a notebook of his bird observations and his younger sister Sophia maintained an herbarium of wild flowers most of her life.

Love of nature was, and still is, a tradition in Massachusetts. Every town had its local amateur experts on flowers or trees or birds or insects. (In the town in which I grew up, not far from Concord, a hundred years later, the local street cleaner had a collection of nearly two hundred species of bird skins and reported regularly to the Smithsonian Institution in Washington on his field observations.) Many towns (Concord among them) maintained public "cabinets of natural history" containing specimens of local flora, fauna, geology, and Indian implements. Concord, through its Lyceum, sponsored frequent lectures on natural history. Thoreau in later years often lectured there himself on such subjects.

What is more, the later 1830s and 1840s saw a great surge of interest in natural history. The Commonwealth of Massachusetts commissioned and then published a whole series of reports on the birds, mammals, fish, reptiles, and herbaceous plants of the state. Thoreau reviewed the whole series for the *Dial* in 1842 and then kept them in his personal library for ready reference. The earliest field guides to American flora and fauna were just appearing. Thoreau acquired many of these and supplemented them with British field guides when American guides were not available. Natural history societies were also just coming into being. Thoreau became an honorary member of the Boston Natural History

Society in 1850 and remained active in it the remainder of his life. Many of his personal collections of specimens were given to the Society by his family after his death. And perhaps most important of all, men such as Louis Agassiz, Asa Gray, and Thaddeus William Harris were at the peak of their careers in identifying and classifying American flora and fauna. Thoreau collected specimens for Agassiz and maintained a long friendship with Harris.

Thoreau was generally considered an eccentric by his fellow Concordians because, though college educated, he refused to follow any profession and because for two years he lived alone in a cabin in the woods at Walden Pond. Typical of the attitude of many Concordians toward him was that of a farmer by the name of Murray. Mrs. Daniel Chester French, the wife of Concord's sculptor, tells of Murray's comments:

I went out in my field across there to the river,
and there, beside that little old mud pond, was
standing Da-a-vid Henry, and he wasn't doin'
nothin' but just standin' there—lookin' at that
pond, and when I came back at noon, there
he was standin' with his hands behind him just
lookin' down into that pond, and after dinner
when I came back again, if there wasn't Da-
a-vid standin' there just like as if he had been
there all day, gazin' down into that pond, and
I stopped and looked at him and I says, "Da-
a-vid Henry, what air you a-doin?" And he
didn't turn his head and he didn't look at me.
He kept lookin' down at that pond, and he
said, as if he was thinkin' about the stars in
the heavens, "Mr. Murray, I'm a-studyin'—
the habits—of the bullfrog!" And there that
darned fool had been standin'—the live-long
day—a-studyin *—the habits—of the* bull-frog![1]

But Thoreau gradually won his fellow townsmen's respect for his knowledge of natural history.
First children of the town and then later the adults
began asking him about unusual specimens they
came across, often donating the specimens to his
collections. His friend Bronson Alcott (father of
Louisa May of *Little Women* fame) tried to talk the
town fathers into appointing Thoreau Concord's of-
ficial natural historian and even unofficially commissioned him to write a textbook on local natural
history for use in the public schools of Concord
(Alcott was for a time Concord's superintendent of
schools). But at this point, Thoreau was suffering
his final illness and was never able to write the book.

When Thoreau went out into the woods and the fields of Concord, he went well-prepared. Though they were then very much out of style, he wore rough corduroys that would withstand the briars and thorns he often crawled through. His sturdy boots were waterproofed rather than polished. On his head he wore a hat with a special shelf built inside on which to put specimens of rare plants as he found them, maintaining half-jokingly that the vapors rising from his brains kept the plants damp. In his hand he carried a sturdy walking stick with one side flattened and marked off in inches and feet so he could measure specimens in the field accurately. In his pocket was a notebook and pencil with which he could make preliminary notes for his journal. At the appropriate times of year, if his afternoon hike was to be a long one, he took along a large music book in which to press leaves and flowers

as soon as he found them. In later years he carried a telescope with him. In bad weather he hooked an umbrella over one arm. Yet all this paraphernalia seemed not to hamper his walking.

His bedroom rapidly became a private museum of the natural history of Concord. After 1850 when his parents acquired the large house on Main Street where he and they lived for the remainders of their lives, he used the whole attic as his bedroom. Shelves, often built from driftwood gathered on his boating excursions on Concord's rivers, were everywhere. They held his books, his specimens of birds' eggs and nests, insects, arrowheads, pressed plants and flowers, shells, and anything unusual he came across in his wanderings. His sister Sophia complained that he didn't dust his shelves as often as she would like, but Henry was not particularly interested in competing with Concord housewives for housekeeping honors. If visitors wished to see his specimens they could easily enough blow off the dust.

Not all of Thoreau's explorations were afoot. Concord boasted of three rivers—the Assabet, the Concord, and the Sudbury—as well as Walden Pond, White's Pond, the Goose Ponds, Fairhaven Bay (an enlargement of the Sudbury River), and numerous smaller ponds. Thoreau was handy with tools and built a whole series of boats over the years which he kept at Walden Pond or on the rivers. He was a superb oarsman who could scull skillfully standing up as well as row. Nathaniel Hawthorne, who, while living in Concord's Old Manse, once bought one of Thoreau's boats, was convinced Thoreau could will his boats to go where he wanted them without touching an oar. In the winter Thoreau often took his excursions on the river ice and would skate as much as twenty or thirty miles in an afternoon. In warm weather he would take what he

liked to call "fluviatile excursions," wading up and down the rivers nude, wearing only a hat for protection from the sun. In deference to Victorian sensibilities, he confined most of those excursions to the more secluded Assabet River. Why he did not lose a toe or other important appendage to snapping turtles, always prevalent in the Concord rivers, is a wonder.

Another favorite excursion was what he called a bee-line hike (more recently popular as orienteering). Picking out a destination on a map or on the distant horizon, he would set his compass for it and then start out in a straight line no matter what was in the way. If it were a hill, he would climb it; a pond, he would swim it. Tradition says that on one occasion he found a house in the way, but since it was a hot summer day and both front and back doors were open, he simply marched through the house, leaving the owners, eating their dinner at the moment, gaping in astonishment.

Thoreau took most of his walks alone by choice. In later years especially he was bombarded with requests from his friends and strangers to accompany him. But he found their company a distraction for they were usually more interested in talking than in observing nature. So when he could do so, sometimes with little grace, he denied their requests. Friends such as H.G.O. Blake of Worcester or Daniel Ricketson of New Bedford or John L. Russell of Salem, who he knew were genuinely interested in natural history, he would permit to accompany him; particularly since their homes were at a distance from Concord, and their requests would not come too often. The one real exception to the rule was Ellery Channing. Channing, almost exactly Thoreau's age, was a member of a prominent Boston family. A ne'er-do-well himself, he never held any job very long and most of his life permitted his wealthy father to support him. He dabbled in poetry but succeeded in writing few (if any) memorable lines. Eccentric and cranky, he quarreled with almost everyone he knew, including his wife and children and Thoreau's mother who could not abide him. But for some unknown reason he and Thoreau hit it off well and once Channing moved to Concord in 1843, they took innumerable walks together. Channing is only infrequently mentioned in Thoreau's journals, and then usually only as "C," or his presence implied by Thoreau's use of "we," but there is plenty of evidence that Channing was often with Thoreau. Alcott occasionally asked to go along but to

Thoreau's amusement and annoyance, he usually sat down on the first fence rail they came to and preferred to talk rather than walk. Emerson, particularly in the early years, liked to walk with Thoreau, but his ideal was a genteel stroll around Walden Pond rather than the rough tramps through swamps and woods that Thoreau preferred. Thoreau once took Hawthorne out to view his favorite swamp, but Hawthorne eyeing the mosquitoes and snakes wanted only to get out of there as fast as he could. Still another reason for Thoreau's refusal to take many on his walks is that he feared with good reason that widespread knowledge of some of the botanical treasures of Concord might lead to their destruction. Annie Sawyer Downes, who grew up in Concord, tells us that Minot Pratt, another Concord amateur botanist, once showed her a rare plant but told her she should never tell anyone about it because Thoreau had shown it to him and had extracted a promise of secrecy from him so no one would destroy it. Just at that moment, the bushes parted and Thoreau stepped out, chastising Pratt for giving the secret away. But when Pratt pointed out he

had shown Annie the plant to encourage her botanical interest, Thoreau changed his mind and offered to show Annie an even rarer plant, the climbing fern. Over hill and dale, through swamps and across brooks Thoreau took them and finally pointed out the climbing fern. Annie was properly appreciative and when later Pratt asked her if she could find her way back to it, she replied, "After all that walking, never." "I'll tell you another secret then," said Pratt. "The fern was actually only several hundred feet from the plant I showed you!

At times Thoreau thought the Concord landscape too genteel. After all, there were no mountains or virgin timber nearby. The woods were at least second or third growth and with the coming of the railroad to Concord in 1844, even these woods were rapidly disappearing under the woodsman's axe. What was even more discouraging was that so much wildlife had already been "civilized out" of the area. No longer could one hope to find a wolf, moose, beaver, or martin. Thoreau once found an elderly farmer who in his boyhood had seen a deer in the area. He quite rightfully felt that his predecessors in Concord had torn out many pages of the natural history of the area. Paradoxically, when Thoreau visited the then truly wild Maine woods, he found himself not quite at home. Nature there was a little too wild for him and he felt himself a trespasser when he climbed to

Mount Katahdin's peak. He returned to Concord with a realization that what best suited his temperament was the juxtaposition of man and nature he found in his home town.

This juxtaposition with nature he found essential to his life. Any day spent without an excursion into the woods he felt to be a day wasted. And when work at his father's pencil factory at times kept him confined for several days, he began to worry about his health. "In society," he says in his journal entry for December 31, 1941:

> *You will not find health, but in nature. You must converse much with the field and woods, if you would imbibe such health into your mind and spirit as you covet for your body. Society is always diseased, and the best is the sickest. There is no scent in it so wholesome as that of the pines, nor any fragrance so penetrating and restorative as that of everlasting in high pastures. Without that our feet at least stood in the midst of nature, all our faces would be pale and livid.* [2]

Although Thoreau died of tuberculosis at the age of forty-five, it is not at all unlikely that he lived as long as he did only because he spent so much of his time out of doors.

Thoreau developed a reputation among his contemporaries for an uncanny ability to get close to Concord's wildlife. As Ralph Waldo Emerson said in the funeral sermon he preached over Thoreau,

> *His intimacy with animals suggested what*

> *Thomas Fuller records of Butler the apiologist,*
> *that "either he had told the bees things or the*
> *bees had told him." Snakes coiled around his*
> *leg; the fishes swam into his hand, and he took*
> *them out of the water; he pulled the woodchuck*
> *out of his hole by the tail and took the foxes*
> *under his protection from the hunters.*[3]

And Frederick L. Willis, the original of Louisa May
Alcott's Laurie of *Little Women*, records in his
Memoirs a childhood visit to Thoreau at Walden:

> *Suddenly stopping he [Thoreau] said:"Keep*
> *very still and I will show you my family."*
> *Stepping quickly outside the cabin door, he*
> *gave a low and curious whistle; immediate-*
> *ly a woodchuck came running towards him*
> *from a nearby burrow. With varying note, yet*
> *still low and strange, a pair of gray squirrels*
> *were summoned and approached him fearless-*
> *ly. With still another note several birds, in-*
> *cluding two crows, flew towards him, one of*
> *the crows nestling upon his shoulder. I*
> *remember it was the crow resting close to his*
> *head that made the most vivid impression*
> *upon me, knowing how fearful of man this*
> *bird is. He fed them all from his hand, taking*
> *food from his pocket, and petted them gently*
> *before our delightful gaze; and then dismiss-*
> *ed them by different whistling, always strange*
> *and low and short, each little wild thing*
> *departing instantly at hearing its special*
> *signal.*[4]

All this makes a very romantic picture, but I fear it
is more legend than truth. Willis wrote these

recollections seventy years after the fact and Emerson, who could hardly tell a robin from a blue jay, was always overly impressed with Thoreau's abilities as a naturalist. Surely if Thoreau had had those two trained crows at Walden we would have heard report of them from more than one old man romanticizing about his childhood, and besides, it would have been so out of character for Thoreau to thus impose his will on the birds and beasts. Thoreau did have a way with wildlife but he used it to get to know their way of life better and not to impose his way on theirs.

What is more, Thoreau had a sense of humor and was not above pulling the legs of some of his friends when they marveled at his way with the wild. Sometimes he would take some of the more gullible out in his rowboat and suddenly putting his hand into the water, would pull out a live fish! What he would not tell his astonished friends was that he had rowed to the site of a bream's nest he had previously located and, taking advantage of the fact that bream staunchly guard their nests, carefully reached in and caught the fish and then just as carefully returned it to its nest, convincing his friends he had somehow charmed the fish.

All of this is not to say that Thoreau was a charlatan or a fraud. His way with the wild was based on a comprehensive knowledge of the creatures' habits, gained from reading and long hours of patient observation. As he tells us in his journal entry for April 15, 1858, "The naturalist accomplishes a great deal by patience, more perhaps than by activity. He must take his position, and then wait and watch. It is equally true of quadrupeds and reptiles.

Sit still in the midst of their haunts." And this habit of his is confirmed in the little story Abby Hosmer, who as a child had known Thoreau well, once told Raymond Adams:

> *One day. . . we children saw Mr. Thoreau standing right down there across the road near the Assabet. He stood very still, and we knew he was watching something in the water. But we knew we must not disturb him, and so we stayed up here in the dooryard. At noontime he was still there, watching something in the water. And he stayed there all afternoon.*
>
> *At last, though, along about supper time, he came up here to the house. And then we children knew that we'd learn what it was he'd been watching. He'd found a duck that had just hatched out a nest of eggs. She had brought the little ducks down to the water. And Mr. Thoreau had watched all day to see her teach those little ducks about the river.*
>
> *And while we ate our suppers there in the kitchen, he told us the most wonderful stories you ever heard about those ducks.* [5]

And yet it was not just patience that Thoreau used. In the final entry in his journal, November 3, 1861, written only a few months before his death, Thoreau said:

> *After a violent easterly storm in the night, which clears up at noon, I notice that the surface of the railroad causeway, composed of gravel, is singularly marked, as if stratified*

*like some slate rocks, on their edges, so that
I can tell within a small fraction of a degree
from what quarter the rain came. . . . Behind
each little pebble, . . . extends northwest a ridge
of sand an inch or more, which it has protected
from being washed away. . . .*

*All this is perfectly distinct to an observant
eye, and yet could easily pass unnoted by
most.*[6]

As I have said elsewhere:

*[Thoreau] could never take anything for
granted, and looking at the world about him
with a questioning mind, he was constantly
discovering things that others had not noticed.
When from the top of a mountain he noticed
the shadows of clouds in a valley, he quickly
figured how to calculate their height accurately.*

*When he noticed the pattern with which
star fungi split, he puzzled out the reason.
When he observed water squirting through
leaks in a dam, he noticed their varying jets
and reasoned that it was related to the varying heads of water above the leaks.*

*When he discovered that turtles tended to
bury their eggs three inches beneath the soil,
he tested with thermometers and proved that
the overall day and night temperature was
greatest at this depth. And when he noticed that
some of the shingles on his neighbor's roof were
blacker than others, he figured out that those
were the poorer or sappy shingles which ab-*

sorbed the most water in a rainstorm. As his friend and first biographer Ellery Channing said of him, "He was alive from tip to toe with curiosity."[7]

It was patience, an observant eye, and, above all, an inimitable way with words that made Thoreau the nature writer *par excellence*.

Largely (and strangely) overlooked among Thoreau's nature writings are a series of brief essays scattered throughout his journal and never before gathered together. Yet they are among his best pieces of nature writing—not just natural history material with which his journal is replete and brimming, but "adventures with nature," as Edwin Way Teale called them, unique experiences with the flora and fauna of his native Concord. Although they deal with animals no more ferocious than muskrats, woodchucks, or snapping turtles, Thoreau endows them with a sense of adventure, a tension and excitement that, combined with his insights and understanding about wild things, transcends the mere visceral thrill of big game hunting. These essays are not mindless competitions nor sentimental anthropomorphizations, but a celebration of nature through the very faculty that enables humankind to transcend nature—intelligence.

These brief essays vary in length from half a page to at most several pages. As one reads through the full fourteen-volume journal, they stand out like little jewels, obviously polished by the author with an idea approached sometimes half a dozen ways in the same paragraph, Thoreau turning and testing the phrases before our eyes. He probably intended many of them for incorporation into larger essays or books, as his attention to detail (he scrupulously includes scientific names) shows. Indeed, a few of them (the account of the battle of the ants, and his three-dimensional checker game with the loon on Walden Pond) reappear in the text of his masterpiece *Walden*. They are included in this volume because they give the reader the opportunity both of seeing these lesser known early versions and of seeing how Thoreau used journal excerpts as building blocks for his books. Each of these, though brief, is an independent essay and can be enjoyed separately. But their gathering together enhances the delight of each individual piece. Here then are Thoreau's uncollected nature essays from the journal gathered together to be enjoyed.

H.G.O. Blake excerpted much of Thoreau's nature material from the *Journal* as far back as the 1880s in his four seasonal volumes of selections, *Early Spring in Massachusetts* (Boston: Houghton Mifflin, 1881), *Summer* (1884), *Autumn* (1892), and *Winter* (1888), but he concentrated primarily on Thoreau's phenological observations of migrations, flowering season, etc. Bertha Stevens gathered together some more of this material in her *Thoreau: Reporter of the Universe* (New York: John Day, 1939), but based her selection on what would be of most interest to school children. And Charles Anderson, in *Thoreau's World* (Englewood Cliffs: Prentice-Hall, 1971) edited some of the essay material in the *Journal*, but his emphasis was on the belle lettres rather than on particular themes. This is not to denigrate their efforts but simply to point out that their approaches were quite different from mine.

The text of this edition is derived from the fourteen-volume edition of Thoreau's *Journal* edited by Bradford Torrey and Francis H. Allen (Boston: Houghton Mifflin, 1906), which in turn is based on Thoreau's manuscript journal now in the J. Pierpont Morgan Library in New York City. The Torrey-Allen edition is a slightly regularized literal transcription of the manuscript, with all additions and corrections added within square brackets. The editor of this volume has followed the same pattern and has added a few identifications, again always within square brackets. Thoreau himself occasionally questions some of his entries by adding a question mark between parentheses. Torrey and Allen occasionally question Thoreau's handwriting by adding a question mark between square brackets.

Thoreau's early journal is often fragmentary because he "mined" it regularly for material for his early books and essays. Therefore many of the early entries (that is, up to about 1850) are undated. In this edition we have adopted the approximate datings of Torrey and Allen in such cases.

In recounting his adventures in nature, Thoreau often mentions friends, acquaintances, and fellow

townsmen without giving full names. These names have been included in square brackets in cases where the names are known. It may be of interest that the "C" occasionally mentioned is his closest friend and later biographer W. Ellery Channing and Blake is Harrison G.O. Blake, his Worcester correspondent and disciple. Those curious about the various natural history books that Thoreau occasionally mentions are referred to Walter Harding's *Thoreau's Library* (Charlottesville: University of Virginia Press, 1957; revised, 1983).

Because Thoreau often discussed a number of topics in any one day's entry, we have occasionally used excerpts rather than full entries. Such excerpting has been indicated only when we have elided words *within* what we have quoted, and there the elisions have been indicated by the use of ellipses.

1. Mrs. Daniel Chester French, *Memories of a Sculptor's Wife,* (Boston: Houghton Mifflin, 1928), pp. 94-95.

2. Henry David Thoreau, *Journal,* (Boston: Houghton Mifflin, 1906), I, pp. 306-307.

3. Ralph Waldo Emerson, *The Complete Works of Ralph Waldo Emerson,* (Boston: Houghton Mifflin, 1903), X, p.472.

4. Frederick Willis, *Alcott Memories,* (Boston: Badgea, 1913), pp. 91-92.

5. Quoted in Raymond Adams, "Thoreau and His Neighbors," *Thoreau Society Bulletin,* 64, p. 4.

6. Henry David Thoreau, *Journal,* (Boston: Houghton Mifflin, 1906), XIV, p. 346.

7. Walter Harding, *The Days of Henry Thoreau,* (New York: Knopf, 1965), pp. 355-356.

IN THE WOODS AND FIELDS OF CONCORD

October 29, 1837. Two ducks, of the summer or wood species, which were merrily dabbling in their favorite basin, struck up a retreat on my approach, and seemed disposed to take French leave, paddling off with swan-like majesty. They are first-rate swimmers, beating me at a round pace, and—what was to me a new trait in the duck character—[they] dove every minute or two and swam several feet under water, in order to escape our attention. Just before immersion they seemed to give each other a significant nod, and then, as if by a common understanding, 't was heels up and head down in the shaking of a duck's wing. When they reappeared, it was amusing to observe with what a self-satisfied, darn-it-how-he-nicks-'em air they paddled off to repeat the experiment.

January 30, 1841. Fair Haven pond is *scored* with the trails of foxes, and you may see where they have gambolled and gone through a hundred evolutions, which testify to a singular listlessness and leisure in nature.

Suddenly, looking down the river, I saw a fox some sixty rods off, making across to the hills on my left. As the snow lay five inches deep, he made but slow progress, but it was no impediment to me.

So, yielding to the instinct of the chase, I tossed my head aloft and bounded away, snuffing the air like a fox-hound, and spurning the world and the Humane Society at each bound. It seemed the woods rang with the hunter's horn, and Diana and all the satyrs joined in the chase and cheered me on. Olympian and Elean youths were waving palms on the hills. In the meanwhile I gained rapidly on the fox; but he showed a remarkable presence of mind, for, instead of keeping up the face of the hill, which was steep and unwooded in that part, he kept along the slope in the direction of the forest, though he lost ground by it. Notwithstanding his fright, he took no step which was not beautiful. The course on his part was a series of most graceful curves. It was a sort of leopard canter, I should say, as if he were nowise impeded by the snow, but were husbanding his strength all the while. When he doubled I wheeled and cut him off, bounding with fresh vigor, and Antaeus-like, recovering my strength each time I touched the snow. Having got near enough for a fair view, just as he was slipping into the wood, I gracefully yielded him the palm. He ran as though there were not a bone in his back, occasionally dropping his muzzle to the snow for a rod or two, and then tossing his head aloft when satisfied of his course. When he came to a declivity he put his fore feet together and slid down it like a cat. He trod so softly that you could not have heard it from any nearness, and yet with such expression that it would not have been quite inaudible at any distance. So, hoping this experience would prove a useful lesson to him, I returned to the village by the highway of the river.

*1*845. There are scores of pitch pines in my field [at Walden], from one to three inches in diameter, girdled by the mice last winter. A Norwegian winter it was for them, for the snow lay long and deep, and they had to mix much pine meal with their usual diet. Yet these trees have not many of them died, even in midsummer, and laid bare for a foot, but have grown a foot. They seem to do all their gnawing beneath the snow. There is not much danger of the mouse tribe becoming extinct in hard winters, for their granary is a cheap and extensive one.

Here is one has had her nest under my house, and came when I took my luncheon to pick the crumbs at my feet. It had never seen the race of man before, and so the sooner became familiar. It ran over my shoes and up my pantaloons inside, clinging to my flesh with its sharp claws. It would run up the side of the room by short impulses like a squirrel, which [it] resembles, coming between the house mouse and the former. Its belly is a little reddish, and its ears a little longer. At length, as I leaned my elbow on the bench, it ran over my arm and round the paper which contained my dinner. And when I held it a piece of cheese, it came and nibbled between my fingers, and then cleaned its face and paws like a fly.

*A**ugust, 1845.* And then the frogs, bullfrogs; they are the more sturdy spirits of ancient wine-bibbers and wassailers, still unrepentant, trying to sing a catch in the Stygian lakes. They would fain keep up the hilarious good fellowship and all the rules of their old round tables, but they have waxed hoarse and solemnly grave and serious their voices, mocking at mirth, and their wine has lost its flavor and is only liquor to distend their paunches, and never comes sweet intoxication to drown the memory of the past, but mere saturation and water-logged dullness and distension. Still the most aldermanic, with his chin upon a pad, which answers for a napkin to his drooling chaps, under the eastern shore quaffs a deep draught of the once scorned water, and passes round the cup with the ejaculation *tr-r-r-r-r-oonk, tr-r-r-r-r-oonk, tr-r-r-r-oonk!* and straightway comes over the water from some distant cove the selfsame password, where the next in seniority and girth has gulped down to his mark; and when the strain has made the circuit of the shores, then ejaculates the master of ceremonies with satisfaction *tr-r-r-r-oonk!* and each in turn repeats the sound, down to the least distended, leakiest, flabbiest paunched, that there be no mistake; and the bowl goes round again, until the sun dispels the morning mist and only the patriarch is not under the pond, but vainly bellowing *troonk* from time to time, pausing for a reply.

1845-1847. The loon comes in the fall to sail and bathe in the pond, making the woods ring with its wild laughter in the early morning, at rumor of whose arrival all Concord sportsmen are on the alert, in gigs, on foot, two by two, three [by three], with patent rifles, patches, conical balls, spy-glass or open hole over the barrel. They seem already to hear the loon laugh; come rustling through the woods like October leaves, these on this side, those on that, for the poor loon cannot be omnipresent; if he dive here, [he] must come up somewhere. The October wind rises, rustling the leaves, ruffling the pond water, so that no loon can be seen rippling the surface. Our sportsmen scour, sweep the pond with spy-glass in vain, making the woods ring with rude [?] charges of powder, for the loon went off in that morning rain with one loud, long, hearty laugh, and our sportsmen must beat a retreat to town and stable and daily routine, shop work, unfinished jobs again.

February 22. [no year] Jean Lapin [the rabbit] sat at my door to-day, three paces from me, at first trembling with fear, yet unwilling to move; a poor, wee thing, lean and bony, with ragged ears

and sharp nose, scant tail and slender paws. It looked as if nature no longer contained the breed of
nobler bloods, the earth stood on its last legs. Is
nature, too, unsound at last? I took two steps, and
lo, away he scud[ded] with elastic spring over the

snowy crust into the bushes, a free creature of the
forest, still wild and fleet; and such then was his
nature, and his motion asserted its vigor and digni-
ty. Its large eye looked at first young and diseased,
almost dropsical, unhealthy. But it bound[ed] free,
the venison, straightening of its body and its limbs
into graceful length, and soon put the forest between me and itself.

*1*837-1847. Yesterday I skated after a fox over
the ice. Occasionally he sat on his haunches and
barked at me like a young wolf. It made me think
of the bear and her cubs mentioned by Captain
Parry, I think. All brutes seem to have a genius
for mystery, an Oriental aptitude for symbols
and the language of signs; and this is the origin
of Pilpay and Aesop. The fox manifested an almost
human suspicion of mystery in my actions. While
I skated directly after him, he cantered at the top
of his speed; but when I stood still, though his fear
was not abated, some strange but inflexible law of

his nature caused him to stop also, and sit again on his haunches. While I still stood motionless, he would go slowly a rod to one side, then sit and bark, then a rod to the other side, and sit and bark again, but did not retreat, as if spellbound. When, however, I commenced the pursuit again, he found himself released from his durance.

Plainly the fox belongs to a different order of things from that which reigns in the village. Our courts, though they offer a bounty for his hide, and our pulpits, though they draw many a moral from his cunning, are in few senses contemporary with his free forest life.

1850. I have been surprised to discover the amount and the various kinds of life which a single shallow swamp will sustain. On the south side of the pond, not more than a quarter of a mile from it, is a small meadow of ten or a dozen acres in the woods, considerably lower than Walden, and which by some is thought to be fed by the former by a subterranean outlet,—which is very likely, for its shores are quite springy and its supply of water is abundant and unfailing,—indeed tradition says that a sawmill once stood over its outlet, though its whole extent, including its sources, is not more than I have mentioned,—a meadow through which the Fitchburg Railroad passes by a very high causeway, which required many a carload of sand, where the laborers for a long time seemed to make no progress, for the sand settled so much in the night that by morning they were where they were the day before, and finally the weight of the sand forced upward the adjacent crust of the meadow with the trees on it many feet, and cracked it for some rods around. It is a wet and springy place throughout the summer, with a ditch-like channel, and in one part water stands the year round, with cat-o'-nine-tails and tussocks and muskrats' cabins rising above it, where good cranberries may be raked if you are careful to anticipate the frost which visits this cool hollow unexpectedly early. Well, as I was saying, I heard a splashing in the shallow and muddy water and stood awhile to observe the cause of it. Again and again I heard and saw the commotion, but could not guess the cause of it,—what kind of life had its residence in that insignificant pool. We sat down on the hillside. Ere long a muskrat came swimming by as if attracted by the same disturbance, and then another and another, till three had passed, and I began to suspect that they were at the bottom of it. Still ever and anon I observed the same commotion in the waters over the same spot, and at length I observed the snout of some creature slyly raised above the surface after each commotion, as if to see if it were observed by foes, and then but a few rods distant I saw another snout above the water and began to divine the cause of the disturbance. Putting off my shoes and stockings, I crept stealthily down the hill and waded out slowly and noiselessly about a rod from the firm land, keeping behind the tussocks, till I stood behind the tussock near which I had observed the splashing. Then, suddenly stooping over it, I saw through the shallow but muddy water that there was a mud turtle there, and thrusting in my hand at once caught him by the claw, and quicker than I can tell it, heaved him high and dry ashore; and there came out with him a large

pout [fish] just dead and partly devoured, which he held in his jaws. It was the pout in his flurry and the turtle in his struggles to hold him fast which had created the commotion. There he had lain, probably buried in the mud at the bottom up to his eyes, till the pout came sailing over, and then this musky lagune had put forth in the direction of his ventral fins, expanding suddenly under the influence of a more than vernal heat,—there are sermons in stones, aye and mud turtles at the bottoms of the pools,— in the direction of his ventral fins, his tender white belly, where he kept no eye; and the minister squeaked his last. Oh, what an eye was there, my countrymen! buried in mud up to the lids, meditating on what? sleepless at the bottom of the pool, at the top of the bottom, directed heavenward, in no danger from motes. Pouts expect their foes

not from below. Suddenly a mud volcano swallowed him up, seized his midriff; he fell into those
relentless jaws from which there is no escape, which
relax not their hold even in death. There the pout
might calculate on remaining until nine days after
the head was cut off. Sculled through Heywood's
shallow meadow, not thinking of foes, looking
through the water up into the sky. I saw his [the
turtle's] brother sunning and airing his broad back
like a ship bottom up which had been scuttled,—
foundered at sea. I had no idea that there was so
much going on in Heywood's meadow.

November 24, 1850. I saw a muskrat come out
of a hole in the ice. He is a man wilder than Ray
or Melvin [two Concord hunters]. While I am looking at him, I am thinking what he is thinking of me.
He is a different sort of a man, that is all. He would
dive when I went nearer, then reappear again, and
had kept open a place five or six feet square so that
it had not frozen, by swimming about in it. Then
he would sit on the edge of the ice and busy himself
about something, I could not see whether it was a
clam or not. What a cold-blooded fellow! thoughts
at a low temperature, sitting perfectly still so long
on ice covered with water, mumbling a cold, wet
clam in its shell. What safe, low, moderate thoughts
it must have! It does not get on to stilts. The generations of muskrats do not fail. They are not preserved by the legislature of Massachusetts.

August 20, 1851. I hear a cricket in the Depot
Field, walk a rod or two, and find the note
proceeds from near a rock. Partly under a rock, between it and the roots of the grass, he lies con-

cealed, — for I pull away the withered grass with my hands,—uttering his night-like creak, with a vibratory motion of his wings, and flattering himself that it is night, because he has shut out the day. He was a black fellow nearly an inch long, with two long, slender feelers. They plainly avoid the light and hide their heads in the grass. At any rate they regard this as the evening of the year. They are remarkably secret and unobserved, considering how much noise they make. Every milkman has heard them all his life; it is the sound that fills his ears as he drives along. But what one has ever got off his cart to go in search of one? I see smaller ones moving stealthily about, whose note I do not know. Who ever distinguished their various notes, which fill the crevices in each other's song? It would be a curious ear, indeed, that distinguished the species of the crickets which it heard, and traced even the earth-song home, each part to its particular performer. I am afraid to be so knowing. They are shy as birds, these little bodies. Those nearest me continually cease their song as I walk, so that the singers

are always a rod distant, and I cannot easily detect one. It is difficult, moreover, to judge correctly whence the sound proceeds. Perhaps this wariness is necessary to save them from insectivorous birds, which would otherwise speedily find out so loud a singer. They are somewhat protected by the universalness of the sound, each one's song being merged and lost in the general concert, as if it were the creaking of earth's axle. They are very numerous in oats and other grain, which conceals them and yet affords a clear passage. I never knew any drought or sickness so to prevail as to quench the song of the crickets; it fails not in its season, night or day.

*A**ugust 22, 1851.*** I saw a snake by the roadside and touched him with my foot to see if he were alive. He had a toad in his jaws, which he was preparing to swallow with his jaws distended to three times his width, but he relinquished his prey in haste and fled; and I thought, as the toad jumped leisurely away with his slime-covered hind-quarters glistening in the sun, as if I, his deliverer, wished to interrupt his meditations,—without a shriek or fainting,—I thought what a healthy indifference he manifested. Is not this the broad earth still? he said.

*D*ecember 30, 1851. This afternoon, being on Fair Haven Hill, I heard the sound of a saw, and soon after from the Cliff saw two men sawing down a noble pine beneath, about forty rods off. I resolved to watch it till it fell, the last of a dozen or more which were left when the forest was cut and for fifteen years have waved in solitary majesty over the sprout-land. I saw them like beavers or insects gnawing at the trunk of this noble tree, the diminutive manikins with their cross-cut saw which could scarcely span it. It towered up a hundred feet as I afterward found by measurement, one of the tallest probably in the township and straight as an arrow, but slanting a little toward the hillside, its top seen against the frozen river and the hills of Conantum. I watch closely to see when it begins to move. Now the sawers stop, and with an axe open it a little on the side toward which it leans, that it may break the faster. And now their saw goes again. Now surely it is going; it is inclined one quarter of the quadrant, and, breathless, I expect its crashing fall. But no, I was mistaken; it has not moved an inch; it stands at the same angle as at first. It is fifteen minutes yet to its fall. Still its branches wave in the wind, as if it were destined to stand for a century, and the wind soughs through its needles as of yore; it is still a forest tree, the most majestic tree that waves over Musketaquid. The silvery sheen of the sunlight is reflected from its needles; it still affords an inaccessible crotch for the squirrel's nest; not a lichen has forsaken its mast-like stem, its raking mast,—the hill is the hulk. Now, now's the moment! The manikins at its base are fleeing from their crime. They have dropped the guilty saw and axe.

How slowly and majestically it starts! as if it were only swayed by a summer breeze, and would return without a sigh to its location in the air. And now it fans the hillside with its fall, and it lies down to its bed in the valley, from which it is never to rise, as softly as a feather, folding its green mantle about it like a warrior, as if, tired of standing, it embraced the earth with silent joy, returning its elements to

the dust again. But hark! there you only saw, but did not hear. There now comes up a deafening crash to these rocks, advertising [to] you that even trees do not die without a groan. It rushes to embrace the earth, and mingle its elements with the dust. And now all is still once more and forever, both to eye and ear.

I went down and measured it. It was about four feet in diameter where it was sawed, about one hundred feet long. Before I had reached it the axemen had already half divested it of its branches. Its gracefully spreading top was a perfect wreck on the hillside as if it had been made of glass, and the tender cones of one year's growth upon its summit appealed in vain and too late to the mercy of the chopper. Already he has measured it with his axe, and marked off the mill-logs it will make. And the space it occupied in upper air is vacant for the next two centuries. It is lumber. He has laid waste the air. When the fish hawk in the spring revisits the banks of the Musketaquid, he will circle in vain to find his accustomed perch, and the hen-hawk will mourn for the pines lofty enough to protect her brood. A plant which it has taken two centuries to perfect, rising by slow stages into the heavens, has this afternoon ceased to exist. Its sapling top had expanded to this January thaw as the forerunner of summers to come. Why does not the village bell sound a knell? I hear no knell tolled. I see no procession of mourners in the streets, or the woodland aisles. The squirrel has leaped to another tree; the hawk has circled further off, and has now settled upon a new eyrie, but the woodman is preparing [to] lay his axe at the root of that also.

January 21, 1852. One day, when I went out to my wood-pile, or rather my pile of stumps, I observed two large ants, the one red, the other much larger and black, fiercely contending with one another, and rolling over on the chips. It was evidently a struggle for life and death which had grown out of a serious feud. Having once got hold, they never let go of each other, but struggled and wrestled and rolled on the chips, each retaining his hold with mastiff-like pertinacity. Looking further, I found to my astonishment that the chips were covered with such combatants, that it was not a *duellum* but a *bellum,* a war between two races of ants, the red always pitted against the black, and frequently two red ones to one black. They covered all the hills and vales of my wood-yard, and, indeed, the ground was already strewn with the dead, both red and black. It was the only war I had ever witnessed, the only battle-field I ever trod while the battle was raging; internecine war; the red republicans and the black despots or imperialists. On every side they were engaged in deadly combat, yet without any noise that I could hear, and never human soldiers fought so resolutely. I watched a couple, in a little sunny valley amid the chips, that were fast locked in each other's embraces, now at noonday prepared to fight till the sun went down. The smaller red champion had fastened himself like a vise to his adversary's front, and through all the tumblings on that field never for an instant ceased to gnaw at one of his feelers near the root, having already caused the other to go by the board, while the stronger black one dashed him from side to side, and, as I saw on looking nearer, had divested him of several of his members. None manifested a disposition to retreat from the combat equal or unequal. It was evident that their battle-cry was conquer or die. They fought like mastiffs or bulldogs, who will not let go though

all their legs are cut off. In the meanwhile there came along a single red ant on the side-hill of this valley, evidently full of excitement, who either had dispatched his foe or had not yet taken part in the battle; probably the latter, for he had lost none of his limbs. He saw this unequal combat from afar, — for the blacks were nearly twice the size of the red, — he drew near with rapid pace till he stood on his guard within half an inch of the combatants, then, watching his opportunity, he sprang upon the black warrior and commenced his operations near the root of his right fore leg, leaving the other to select among his own members, and so there were three united for life and death apparently, — united for life until death, — as if a new kind of attraction had been invented, which put all other locks and cements to shame.

I should not wonder if they had their respective musical bands stationed on some chip and playing their national airs the while to cheer the dying combatants. (Whose mother had charged him to return with his shield or upon it.) I was myself excited somewhat, even as if they had been men. The more you think of it, the less the difference. And certainly there is no other fight recorded in Concord that will bear a moment's comparison with this. I have no doubt they had as just a cause, one or even both parties, as our forefathers, and that the results will be as important and memorable. And there was far more patriotism and heroism. For numbers and for carnage it was an Austerlitz or Dresden. I saw no disposition to retreat.

I took up the chip on which the three I have particularly described were struggling, carried it into my house, and placed it under a tumbler on my window-sill, wishing [to] see the issue. Holding a microscope to the first-mentioned red ant, I saw that though he was assiduously gnawing at the near fore leg of his enemy, having severed his remaining feeler, his own breast was all torn away, exposing what vitals he had there to the jaws of the black warrior, whose own breastplate was apparently too thick for him; and the dark carbuncles of his eyes shone with ferocity such as wars only could excite. They struggled for half an hour longer under the tumbler, and when I looked again, the black soldier had severed the heads of his foes from their bodies, and the former were hanging on either side of him still apparently as firmly fastened as ever, and he was endeavoring, with feeble struggles, and I know not how many other wounds, to divest himself of them; which at length, after half an hour more, he had accomplished. I raised the tumbler, and he went off over the window-sill in that crippled state. Whether he finally survived that combat and had a pension settled on him, I do not know. But I thought that his industry would not be worth much thereafter.

Which party was victorious I never learned, nor the cause of the war. But I felt for the rest of that day as if I had had my feelings harrowed and ex-

cited by witnessing the struggle, the ferocity and carnage, of a human battle before my door.

*F*ebruary 20, 1852. P.M.—To Flint's Pond.
The last two or three days have been *among*
the coldest in the winter, though not so cold as a
few weeks ago. I notice, in the low ground covered
with bushes near Flint's Pond, many little rabbit-
paths in the snow, where they have travelled in each
other's tracks, or many times back and forth, six inches wide. This, too, is probably their summer habit.
The rock by the pond is remarkable for its um-
bilicaria (?).

I saw a mole (?) run along under the bank by
the edge of the pond, but it was only by watching
long and sharply that I glimpsed him now and then,
he ran so close to the ground and under rather than
over anything, as roots and beds of leaves and twigs,
and yet without making any noise. No wonder that
we so rarely see these animals, though their tracks
are so common. I have been astonished to observe
before, after holding them in my hand, how quickly they will bury themselves and glide along just
beneath the surface, whatever it may be composed
of,—grass or leaves or twigs or earth or snow. So
some men are sly and subterranean in their ways,
and skulk, though often they raise a mound of earth
or snow above their backs, which betrays rather
than conceals them. For privacy they prefer to travel
in a gallery like the mole, though it sometimes hap-
pens that it is arched above the ground when they
think themselves deep in the sod. The mole goes
behind and beneath, rather than before and above.

*A*pril *16, 1852.* As I turned round the corner of Hubbard's Grove, [I] saw a woodchuck, the first of the season, in the middle of the field, six or seven rods from the fence which bounds the wood, and twenty rods distant. I ran along the fence and cut him off, or rather overtook him, though he started at the same time. When I was only [a] rod and a half off, he stopped, and I did the same; then he ran again, and I ran up within three feet of him, when he stopped again, the fence being between us. I squatted down and surveyed him at my leisure. His eyes were dull black and rather inobvious, with a faint chestnut (?) iris, with but little expression and that more of resignation than of anger. The general aspect was a coarse grayish brown, a sort of grisel (?). A lighter brown next the skin, then black or very dark brown and tipped with whitish rather loosely. The head between a squirrel and a bear, flat on the top and dark brown, and darker still or black on the tip of the nose. The whiskers black, two inches long. The ears very small and roundish, set far back and nearly buried in the fur. Black feet, with long and slender claws for digging. It appeared to tremble, or perchance shivered with cold. When I moved, it.gritted its teeth quite loud, sometimes striking the under jaw against the other chatteringly, sometimes grinding one jaw on the other, yet as if more from instinct than anger. Whichever way I turned, that way it headed. I took a twig a foot long and touched its snout, at which it started forward and bit the stick, lessening the distance between us to two feet, and still it held all the ground it gained. I played with it tenderly awhile with the`stick, trying to open its gritting jaws. Ever its long incisors, two above and two below, were presented. But I thought it would go to sleep if I stayed long enough. It did not sit upright as sometimes, but *standing* on its fore feet with its head down, *i.e.* half sitting, half standing. We sat looking at one another about half an hour, till we began to feel mesmeric influences. When I was tired,

I moved away, wishing to see him run, but I could not start him. He would not stir as long as I was looking at him or could see him. I walked round him; he turned as fast and fronted me still. I sat down by his side within a foot. I talked to him *quasi* forest lingo, baby-talk, at any rate in a conciliatory tone, and thought that I had some influence on him. He gritted his teeth less. I chewed checkerberry leaves and presented them to his nose at last without a grit; though I saw that by so much gritting of the teeth he had worn them rapidly and they were covered with a fine white powder, which, if you measured it thus, would have made his anger terrible. He did not mind any noise I might make. With a little stick I lifted one of his paws to examine it, and held it up at pleasure. I turned him over to see what color he was beneath (darker or more purely brown), though he turned himself back again sooner than I could have wished. His tail was also all brown, though not very dark, rat-tail like, with loose hairs standing out on all sides like a caterpillar brush. He had a rather mild look. I spoke kindly to him. I reached checkerberry leaves to his mouth. I stretched my hands over him, though he turned up his head and still gritted a little. I laid my hand on him, but immediately took it off again, instinct not being wholly overcome. If I had had a few fresh bean leaves, thus in advance of the season, I am sure I should have tamed him completely. It was a frizzly tail. His is a humble, terrestrial color like the partridge's, well concealed where dead wiry grass rises above darker brown or chestnut dead leaves,—a modest color. If I had had some food, I should have ended with stroking him at my leisure. Could easily have wrapped him in my handkerchief. He was not fat nor particularly lean. I finally had to leave him without seeing him move from the place. A large, clumsy, burrowing squirrel. *Arctomys,* bearmouse. I respect him as one of the natives. He lies there, by his color and habits so naturalized amid the dry leaves, the withered grass, and the bushes. A sound nap, too, he has enjoyed in his native fields, the past winter. I think I might learn some wisdom of him. His ancestors have lived here longer than mine. He is more thoroughly acclimated and naturalized than I. Bean leaves the red man raised for him, but he can do without them.

A ***pril 18, 1852.*** Going through Dennis's field with C. [Ellery Channing], saw a flock of geese on east side of river near willows. Twelve great birds on the troubled surface of the meadow, delayed by the storm. We lay on the ground behind an oak and our umbrella, eighty rods off, and

watched them. Soon we heard a gun go off, but
could see no smoke in the mist and rain. And the
whole flock rose, spreading their great wings and
flew with clangor a few rods and lit in the water
again, then swam swiftly toward our shore with outstretched necks. I knew them first from ducks by
their long necks. Soon appeared the man, running

toward the shore in vain, in his greatcoat; but he soon retired in vain. We remained close under our umbrella by the tree, ever and anon looking through a peep-hole between the umbrella and the tree at the birds. On they came, sometimes in two, sometimes in three, squads, warily, till we could see the steel-blue and green reflections from their necks. We held the dog close the while, — C., lying on his back in the rain, had him in his arms, — and thus we gradually edged round on the ground in this cold, wet, windy storm, keeping our feet to the tree, and the great wet calf of a dog with his eyes shut so meekly in our arms. We laughed well at our adventure. Occasionally one expanded a gray wing. They showed white on breasts. And not till after half an hour, sitting cramped and cold and wet on the ground, did we leave them.

May 5, 1852. I stand by the bubbling frogs (dreamers at a distance). They are sometimes intermittent, with a quavering. I hear between-whiles a little bird-like conversation between them. It is evidently their wooing.

May 6, 1852. My dream frog turns out to be a toad. I watched half a dozen a long time at 3:30 this afternoon in Hubbard's Pool, where they were frogging (?) lustily. They sat in the shade, either partly in the water, or on a stick; looked darker and narrower in proportion to their length than toads usually do, and moreover are aquatic. I see them jump into the ditches as I walk. After an interval of silence, one appeared to be gulping the wind into his belly, inflating himself so that he was considerably expanded; then he discharged it all into his throat while his body or belly collapsed suddenly, expanding his throat to a remarkable size. Was nearly a minute inflating itself; then swelled out its sac, which is rounded and reminded me of the bag to a worktable, holding its head up the while. It is whitish specked (the bag) on a dull bluish or slate ground, much bigger than all the rest of the head, and nearly an inch in diameter. It was a ludicrous sight, with their so serious prominent eyes peering over it; and a deafening sound, when several were frogging at once, as I was leaning over them. The mouth [seemed] to be shut always, and perhaps the air was expelled through the nostrils. The strain appeared prolonged as long as the air lasted, and was sometimes quavered or made intermittent, apparently by closing the orifice, whatever it was, or the blast. One, which I brought home, answers well enough to the description of the common toad (*Bufo Americanus*), though it is hardly so gray. Their piping (?) was evidently connected with their loves. Close by, it is an unmusical monotonous deafening sound, a steady blast,—not a peep nor a croak, but a *kind* of piping,—but, far away, it is a dreamy, lulling sound, and fills well the crevices of nature. Out of its place, as very near, it would be as intolerable as the thrumming of children. The plower yesterday disturbed a toad in the garden, the first I have heard of. I must catch him and compare them. Their heads are well above the water when they pipe.

Saw a striped snake lying by the roadside as if watching for toads, though they must be scarce now, his head just on the edge of the road. The most flexible of creatures, it is so motionless it appears the most rigid, in its waving line.

July 10, 1852 [Assabet River]. There are but few fishes to be seen. They have, no doubt, retreated to the deepest water. In one somewhat muddier place, close to the shore, I came upon an old pout cruising with her young. She dashed away at my approach, but the fry remained. They were of various sizes from a third of an inch to an inch and a half long, quite black and pout-shaped, except that the head was most developed in the smallest. They were constantly moving about in a somewhat circular, or rather lenticular, school, about fifteen or eighteen inches in diameter, and I estimated that there were at least a thousand of them. Presently the old pout came back and took the lead of her brood, which followed her, or rather gathered about her, like chickens about a hen; but this mother had so many children she didn't know what to do. Her maternal yearnings must be on a great scale. When one half of the divided school found her out, they came down upon her and completely invested her like a small cloud. She was soon joined by another smaller pout, apparently her mate, and all, both old and young, began to be very familiar with me; they came round my legs and felt them with their feelers, and the old pouts nibbled my toes, while the fry half concealed my feet. Probably if I had been standing on the bank with my clothes on they would have been more shy. Ever and anon the old pouts dashed aside to drive away a passing bream or perch. The larger one kept circling about her charge, as if to keep them together within a certain compass. If any of her flock were lost or devoured she could hardly have missed them. I wondered if there was any calling of the roll at night,—whether she, like a faithful shepherdess, ever told her tale under some hawthorn in the river's dales. Ever ready to do battle with the wolves that might break into her fold. The young pouts are protected then for a season by the old. Some had evidently been hatched before the others. One of these large pouts had a large velvet-black spot which included the right pectoral fin, a kind of disease which I have often observed on them.

I wonder if any Roman emperor ever indulged in such luxury as this,—of walking up and down

a river in torrid weather with only a hat to shade the head. What were the baths of Caracalla to this? Now we traverse a long water plain some two feet deep; now we descend into a darker river valley, where the bottom is lost sight of and the water rises to our armpits; now we go over a hard iron pan; now we stoop and go under a low bough of the *Salix nigra;* now we slump into soft mud amid the pads of the *Nymphaea odorata,* at this hour shut. On this road there is no other traveller to turn out for.

September 30, 1852. Thursday. 10 A.M.—To Fair Haven Pond, bee-hunting,—Pratt, Rice, Hastings, and myself, in a wagon. A fine, clear day after the coolest night and severest frost we have had. The apparatus was, first a simple round tin box four and a half inches in diameter and one and a half inches deep, containing a piece of empty honeycomb of its own size and form, filling it within a third of an inch of the top; also another, *wooden* box about two and a half inches square every way, with a glass window occupying two thirds the upper side under a slide, with a couple of narrow slits in the wood, each side of the glass, to admit air, but too narrow for the bees to pass; the whole resting on a circular bottom a little larger than the lid of the tin box, with a sliding door in it. We were earnest to go this week, before the flowers were gone, and we feared the frosty night might make the bees slow to come forth.

After we got to the Baker Farm, to one of the open fields nearest to the tree I had marked, the first thing was to find some flowers and catch some honey-bees. We followed up the bank of the brook for some distance, but the goldenrods were all dried up there, and the asters on which we expected to find them were very scarce. By the pond-side we had no better luck, the frosts perhaps having made flowers still more scarce there. We then took the path to Clematis Brook on the north of Mt. Misery, where we found a few of the *Diplopappus linariifolius* (savory-leaved aster) and one or two small white (bushy?) asters. Also *A. undulatus* and *Solidago nemoralis* rarely, on which they work in a sunny place; but there were only two or three bumblebees, wasps, and butterflies, yellow and small red, on them. We had no better luck at Clematis Brook. Not a honey-bee could we find, and we concluded that we were too late,—that the weather was too cold, and so repaired at once to the tree I had found, a hemlock two feet and a half in diameter on a side-hill a rod from the pond. I had cut my initials in the bark in the winter, for custom gives the first finder of the nest a right to the honey and to cut down the tree to get it and pay the damages, and if he cuts his initials on it no other hunter will interfere. Not seeing any signs of bees from the ground, one of the party climbed the tree to where the leading stem had formerly been broken off, leaving a crotch at about eighteen feet from the ground, and there he found a small hole into which he thrust a stick two or three feet down the tree, and dropped it to the bottom; and, putting in his hand, he took out some old comb. The bees had probably died.

After eating our lunch, we set out on our return. By the roadside at Walden, on the sunny hillside sloping to the pond, we saw a large mass of goldenrod and aster several rods square and comparatively fresh. Getting out of our wagon, we found it to be resounding with the hum of bees. (It was about 1 o'clock.) There were far more flowers than we had seen elsewhere. Here were bees in great numbers, both bumblebees and honey-bees, as well as butterflies and wasps and flies. So, pouring a mixture of honey and water into the empty comb in the tin box, and holding the lid of the tin box in one hand and the wooden box with the slides shut in the other, we proceeded to catch the honey-bees by shutting them in suddenly between the lid of the tin box and the large circular bottom of the wooden one, cutting off the flower-stem with the edge of the lid at the same time. Then, holding the lid still against the wooden box, we drew the slide in the bottom and also the slide covering the window at the top, that the light might attract the bee to pass up into the wooden box. As soon as he had done so and was buzzing against the glass, the lower slide was closed and the lid with the flower removed, and more bees were caught in the same way. Then, placing the other, tin, box containing the comb filled with honeyed water close under the wooden one, the slide was drawn again, and the upper slide closed, making it dark; and in about a minute they went to feeding, as was ascertained by raising slightly the wooden box. Then the latter was wholly removed, and they were left feeding or sucking up the honey in broad daylight. In from two to three minutes one had loaded himself and commenced leaving the box. He would buzz round it back and forth a foot or more, and then, sometimes, finding that he was too heavily loaded, alight to empty himself or clean his feet. Then, starting once more, he would begin to circle round irregularly, at first in a small circle only a foot or two in diameter, as if to examine the premises that he might know them again, till, at length, rising higher and higher and circling wider and wider and swifter and swifter, till his orbit was ten or twelve feet in diameter and as much from the ground,—though its centre might be moved to one side,—so that it was very difficult to follow him, especially if you looked against a wood or the hill, and you had to lie low to fetch him against the sky (you must operate in an open space, not in a wood); all this as if to ascertain the course to his nest; then, in a minute or less from his first starting, he darts off in a bee-line, that is, as far as I could see him, which might be eight or ten rods, looking against the sky (and you had to follow his whole career very attentively indeed to see when and where he went off at a tangent), in a waving or sinuous (right and left) line, toward his nest.

We sent forth as many as a dozen bees, which flew in about three directions, but all toward the village, or where we knew there were hives. They did not fly so almost absolutely straight as I had heard, but within three or four feet of the same course for half a dozen rods, or as far as we could see. Those belonging to one hive all had to digress to get round an apple tree. As none flew in the right direction for us, we did not attempt to line them. In less than half an hour the first returned to the box still lying on the wood-pile,—for not one of the bees on the surrounding flowers discovered it,—and so they came back, one after another, loaded themselves and departed; but now they went off with very little preliminary circling, as if assured of their course. We were furnished with little boxes of red, blue, green, yellow, and white paint, in dry powder, and with a stick we sprinkled a little of the red powder on the back of one while he was feeding,—gave him a little dab,—and it settled down amid the fuzz of his back and gave him a distinct red jacket. He went off like most of them toward some hives about three quarters of a mile distant, and we observed by the watch the time of his departure. In just twenty-two minutes red jacket came back, with enough of the powder still on his back to mark him plainly. He may have gone more than three quarters of a mile. At any rate, he had a head wind to contend with while laden. They fly swiftly and surely to their nests, never resting by the way, and I was surprised—though I had been informed of it—at the distance to which the village bees go for flowers.

The rambler in the most remote woods and pastures little thinks that the bees which are humming so industriously on the rare wild flowers he is plucking for his herbarium, in some out-of-the-way nook, are, like himself, ramblers from the village, perhaps from his own yard, come to get their honey for his hives. All the honey-bees we saw were on the blue-stemmed goldenrod *(Solidago cæsia)*, which is late, lasts long, which emitted a sweet agreeable fragrance, not on the asters. I feel the richer for this experience. It taught me that even the insects in my path are not loafers, but have their special errands. Not merely and vaguely in this world, but in this hour, each is about its business. If, then, there are any sweet flowers still lingering on the hillside, it is known to the bees both of the forest and the village. The botanist should make interest with the bees if he would know when the flowers open and when they close. Those I have named were the only common and prevailing flowers at this time to look for them on.

Our red jacket had performed the voyage in safety; no bird had picked him up. Are the kingbirds gone? Now is the time to hunt bees and take them up, when the combs are full of honey and before the flowers are so scarce that they begin to consume the honey they have stored.

The common milkweed down has begun to fly; the desmodium, tick-trefoil, adheres now to my clothes. Saw by Clematis Brook extensive rootings of moles.

Forty pounds of honey was the most our company had got hereabouts.

We also caught and sent forth a bumblebee, who manœuvred like the others, though we thought he took time to eat some before he loaded himself, and then he was so overloaded and bedaubed that he had to alight after he had started, and it took him several minutes to clean himself.

It is not in vain that the flowers bloom, and bloom late too, in favored spots. To us they are a culture and a luxury, but to bees meat and drink. The tiny bee which we thought lived far away there in a flower-bell in that remote vale, he is a great voyager, and anon he rises up over the top of the wood and sets sail with his sweet cargo straight for his distant haven. How well they know the woods and fields and the haunt of every flower! The flowers, perchance, are widely dispersed, because the sweet which they collect from the atmosphere is rare but also widely dispersed, and the bees are enabled to travel far to find it. A precious burthen, like their color and fragrance, a crop which the heavens bear and deposit on the earth.

O*ctober 8, 1852.* P.M. Walden. As I was paddling along the north shore, after having looked in vain over the pond for a loon, suddenly a loon, sailing toward the middle, a few rods in front, set up his wild laugh and betrayed himself. I pursued with a paddle and he dived, but when he came up I was nearer than before. He dived again, but I miscalculated the direction he would take, and we were fifty rods apart when he came up, and again he laughed long and loud. He managed very cunningly, and I could not get within half a dozen rods of him. Sometimes he would come up unexpectedly on the opposite side of me, as if he had passed directly under the boat. So long-winded was he, so unweariable, that he would immediately plunge again, and then no wit could divine where in the deep pond, beneath the smooth surface, he might be speeding his way like a fish, perchance passing under the boat. He had time and ability to visit the bottom of the pond in its deepest part. A newspaper authority says a fisherman—giving his name—has caught loon in Seneca Lake, N.Y., eighty feet beneath the surface, with hooks set for trout. Miss [Susan F.] Cooper [author of *Rural Hours* (1850)] has said the same. Yet he appeared to know his course as surely under water as on the surface, and swam much faster there than he sailed on the surface. It was surprising how serenely he sailed off with unruffled bosom when he came to the surface. It was as well for me to rest on my oars and await his reappearing as to endeavor to calculate where he would come up. When I was straining my eyes over the surface, I would suddenly be startled by his unearthly laugh behind me. But why, after displaying so much cunning, did he betray himself the moment he came to the surface with that loud laugh? His white breast enough betrayed him. He was indeed a silly loon, I thought. Though he took all this pains to avoid me, he never failed to give notice of his whereabouts the moment he came to the surface. After an hour he seemed as fresh as ever, dived as willingly, and swam yet farther than at first. Once or twice I saw a ripple where he approached the surface, just put his head out to reconnoitre, and instantly dived again. I could commonly hear the plash of the water when he came up, and so also detected him. It was commonly a demoniac laughter, yet somewhat like a water-bird, but occasionally, when he had balked me most successfully and come up a long way off, he uttered a long-drawn unearthly howl, probably more like a wolf than any other bird. This was his looning. As when

a beast puts his muzzle to the ground and deliberately howls; perhaps the wildest sound I ever heard,
making the woods ring; and I concluded that he
laughed in derision of my efforts, confident of his
own resources. Though the sky was overcast, the

pond was so smooth that I could see where he broke the surface if I did not hear him. His white breast, the stillness of the air, the smoothness of the water, were all against [him]. At length, having come up fifty rods off, he uttered one of those prolonged unearthly howls, as if calling on the god of loons to aid him, and immediately there came a wind from the east and rippled the surface, and filled the whole air with misty rain. I was impressed as if it were the prayer of the loon and his god was angry with me. How surprised must be the fishes to see this ungainly visitant from another sphere speeding his way amid their schools!

I have never seen more than one at a time in our pond, and I believe that that is always a male.

October 28, 1852. As I was eating my dinner of rice to-day, with an open window, a small species of wild bee, with many yellow rings about the abdomen, came in and alighted on the molasses pitcher. It took up the molasses quite fast, and soon made quite bare and white a considerable space on the nose of the pitcher which was smeared with molasses; then, having loaded itself, it circled round the pitcher a few times, while I was helping myself to some molasses, and flew against a closed window, but ere long, finding the open one by which it had entered, it winged its way to its nest. Probably if I had been willing to leave the window open and wait awhile, it would have returned.

November 2, 1852, to Walden. In the latter part of October the skaters and waterbugs entirely disappear from the surface of the pond, and then and in November, when the weather is perfectly calm, it is almost absolutely as smooth as glass. This afternoon a three-days' rain-storm is drawing to an end, though still overcast. The air is quite still but misty, from time to time mizzling, and the pond is very smooth, and its surface difficult to distinguish, though it no longer reflects the *bright* tints of autumn but sombre colors only,—calm at the end of a storm, except here and there a slight glimmer or dimple, as if a few skaters which had escaped the frosts were still collected there, or a faint breeze there struck, or a few rain-drops fell there, or perchance the surface, being remarkably smooth, betrayed by circling dimples where a spring welled up from below. I paddled gently toward one of these places and was surprised to find myriads of small perch about five inches long sporting there, one after another rising to the surface and dimpling it, leaving bubbles on it. They were very handsome as they surrounded the boat, with their distinct traverse stripes, a rich brown color. There were many such schools in the pond, as it were improving the short season before the ice would close their window. When I approached them suddenly with noise, they made a sudden plash and rippling with their tails in fright, and then took refuge in the depths. Suddenly the wind rose, the mist increased, and the waves rose, and still the perch leaped, but much higher, half out of water, a hundred black points, three inches long, at once above the surface. The pond, dark before, was now a glorious and indescribable blue, mixed with dark, perhaps the opposite side of the wave, a sort of changeable or watered-silk blue, more cerulean if possible than the sky itself, which was now seen overhead. It required a certain division of the sight, however, to discern this. Like the colors on a steel sword-blade.

*M*arch 6, 1853. Two red squirrels made an ado about or above me near the North River, hastily running from tree to tree, leaping from the extremity of one bough to that of the nearest, or the next tree, until they gained and ascended a large white pine. I approached and stood under this, while they made a great fuss about me. One at length came part way down to reconnoitre me. It seemed that one did the barking—a faint, short, chippy bark, like that of a *toy* dog,—its tail vibrating each time, while its neck was stretched over a bough as it peered at me. The other, higher up, kept up a sort of gurgling whistle, more like a bird than a beast. When I made a noise they would stop a moment.

Scared up a partridge, which had crawled into a pile of wood. Saw a gray hare, a dirty yellowish gray, not trig and neat, but, as usual, apparently in a deshabille. As it frequently does, it ran a little way and stopped just at the entrance to its retreat; then, when I moved again, suddenly disappeared. By a slight obscure hole in the snow, it had access to a large and apparently deep woodchuck's (?) hole.

*M*arch 27, 1853. Tried to see the faint-croaking frogs at J. P. Brown's Pond in the woods. They are remarkably timid and shy; had their noses and eyes out, croaking, but all ceased, dove, and concealed themselves, before I got within a rod of the shore. Stood perfectly still amid the bushes on the shore, before one showed himself; finally five or six, and all eyed me, gradually approached me within three feet to reconnoitre, and, though I waited about half an hour, would not utter a sound nor take their eyes off me,—were plainly affected by curiosity. Dark brown and some, perhaps, dark green, about two inches long; had their noses and eyes out when they croaked. If described at all, must be either young of *Rana pipiens* or the *R. palustris.*

*M*ay 31, 1853. Some incidents in my life have seemed far more allegorical than actual; they were so significant that they plainly served no other use. That is, I have been more impressed by their allegorical significance and fitness; they have been like myths or passages in a myth, rather than mere incidents or history which have to wait to become significant. Quite in harmony with my subjective philosophy. This, for instance: that, when I thought I knew the flowers so well, the beautiful purple azalea or pinxter-flower should be shown me by the hunter who found it. Such facts are lifted quite above the level of the actual. They are all just such events as my imagination prepares me for, no matter how incredible. Perfectly in keeping with my life and characteristic. Ever and anon something will occur which my philosophy has not dreamed of. The limits of the actual are set some thoughts further off. That which had seemed a rigid wall of vast thickness unexpectedly proves a thin and undulating drapery. The boundaries of the actual are no more fixed and rigid than the elasticity of our imaginations. The fact that a rare and beautiful flower which we never saw,

perhaps never heard [of], for which therefore there was no place in our thoughts, may at length be found in our immediate neighborhood, is very suggestive.

P.M. A change in the weather. It is comparatively cool since last night, and the air is very clear accordingly; none of that haze in it occasioned by the late heat. Yesterday was another very windy day, making the sixth, I believe, of this May, the 23rd having been the last. The leaves are now fairly expanded—that has been the work of May—and are of a dark summer greenness. Some have even begun to cut the rankest grass in front yards. May has been, on the whole, a pleasant month, with a few days of gentle rain-storm,—fishermen's rains,—straight down and spattering on the earth,—and the last

week quite warm, even somewhat sultry and
summer-like. The bulk of the planting has been done
this month, and there have been half a dozen days
of strong, breezy and gusty, but not cold, winds,—
northwest and then southwest and south. It is surprising to see how many leaves are already attack-
ed by insects,—leaf-rollers, pincushion galls, one
kind of oak-balls, etc., etc.; and many a shrub and
tree, black cherry and shrub oak, is no sooner leaved
out than it is completely stripped by its caterpillar
foes.

I am going in search of the *Azalea nudiflora.*
Sophia [Thoreau's sister] brought home a single
flower without twig or leaf from Mrs. [Mary] Brooks'
last evening. Mrs. Brooks, I find, has a large twig
in a vase of water, still pretty fresh, which she says
George Melvin gave to her son George. I called at
his office. He says that Melvin came in to Mr.
Gourgas's office, where he and others were sitting
Saturday evening, with his arms full and gave each
a sprig, but he doesn't know where he got it.
Somebody, I heard, had seen it at Captain Jarvis's;
so I went there. I found that they had some still pretty fresh in the house. Melvin gave it to them Saturday night, but they did not know where he got it.
A young man working at Stedman Buttrick's said it
was a secret; there was only one bush in the town;
Melvin knew of it and Stedman knew; when asked,
Melvin said he got it in the swamp, or from a bush,
etc. The young man thought it grew on the Island
across the river on the Wheeler farm. I went on to
Melvin's house, though I did not expect to find him
at home at this hour, so early in the afternoon. (Saw
the woodsorrel out, a day or two perhaps, by the

way.) At length I saw his dog by the door, and knew he was at home.

He was sitting in the shade, bareheaded, at his back door. He had a large pailful of the azalea recently plucked and in the shade behind his house, which he said he was going to carry to town at evening. He had also a sprig set out. He had been out all the forenoon and said he had got seven pickerel,— perhaps ten [?]. Apparently he had been drinking and was just getting over it. At first he was a little shy about telling me where the azalea grew, but I saw that I should get it out of him. He dilly-dallied a little; called to his neighbor Farmer, whom he called "Razor," to know if he could tell me where that flower grew. He called it, by the way, the "red honeysuckle." This was to prolong the time and make the most of his secret. I felt pretty sure the plant was to be found on Wheeler's land beyond the river, as the young man had said, for I had remembered how, some weeks before this, when

I went up the Assabet after the yellow rocket, I saw Melvin, who had just crossed with his dog, and when I landed to pluck the rocket he appeared out of the woods, said he was after a fish-pole, and asked me the name of my flower. Didn't think it was

very handsome,—"not so handsome as the honeysuckle, is it?" And now I knew it was his "red honeysuckle," and not the columbine, he meant. Well, I told him he had better tell me where it was; I was a botanist and ought to know. But he thought I couldn't possibly find it by his directions. I told him he'd better tell me and have the glory of it, for I should surely find it if he didn't; I'd got a clue to it, and shouldn't give it up. I should go over the river for it. I could smell it a good way, you know. He thought I could smell it half a mile, and he wondered that I hadn't stumbled on it, or Channing. Channing, he said, came close by it once, when it was in flower. He thought he'd surely find it then; but he didn't, and he said nothing to him.

He told me he found it about ten years ago, and he went to it every year. It blossomed at the old election time, and he thought it "the handsomest flower that grows." Yarrow just out.

In the meanwhile, Farmer, who was hoeing, came up to the wall, and we fell into a talk about Dodge's Brook, which runs through his farm. A man in Cambridge, he said, had recently written to Mr. [William] Monroe about it, but he didn't know why. All he knew about the brook was that he had seen it dry and then again, after a week of dry weather in which no rain fell, it would be full again, and either the writer or Monroe said there were only two such brooks in all North America. One of its sources—he thought the principal one—was in his land. We all went to it. It was in a meadow,—rather a dry one, once a swamp. He said it never ceased to flow at the head now, since he dug it out, and never froze there. He ran a pole down eight or nine feet into the mud to show me the depth. He had minnows there in a large deep pool, and cast an insect into the water, which they presently rose to and swallowed. Fifteen years ago he dug it out nine feet deep and found spruce logs as big as his leg, which the beavers had gnawed, with the marks of their teeth very distinct upon them; but they soon crumbled away on coming to the air. Melvin, meanwhile, was telling me of a pair of geese he had seen which were breeding in the Bedford Swamp. He had seen them within a day. Last year he got a large brood (11?) of black ducks there.

We went on down the brook,—Melvin and I and his dog,—and crossed the river in his boat, and he conducted me to where the *Azalea nudiflora* grew,—it was a little past its prime, perhaps,—and showed me how near Channing came. ("You won't tell him what I said; will you?" said he.) I offered to pay him for his trouble, but he wouldn't take anything. He had just as lief I'd know as not. He thought it first came out last Wednesday, on the 25th.

Azalea nudiflora,—purple azalea, pinxter-flower,—but Gray and Bigelow say nothing about its *clamminess*. It is a conspicuously beautiful flowering shrub, with the sweet fragrance of the common swamp-pink, but the flowers are larger and, in this case, a fine lively rosy pink, not so clammy as the other, and, being earlier, it is free from the insects which often infest and spoil the first, though I find a very few little flies on them. With a broader, somewhat downy pale-green leaf. Growing in the shade of large wood, like the laurel. The flowers, being in naked umbels, are so much the more conspicuous. (The *Viola debilis* by the brook, near the azalea.) It is a flower with the fragrance of the swamp[-pink], without its extreme clamminess and consequent insects, and with a high and beautiful color and larger segments to the corolla, with very much exserted stamens and pistil. Eaton says the *nudiflora* is "not viscous;" names half a dozen varieties and among them *A. Partita* (flesh-colored flowers, 5-parted to the base), but then this is viscous. And it cannot be his species *A. nutida*, with glabrous and shining and small leaves. It must be an undescribed variety—a viscous one—of *A. nudiflora.*

June 1, 1853. Walking up this side-hill, I disturbed a nighthawk eight or ten feet from me, which went, half fluttering, half hopping, the mottled creature, like a winged toad, as Nuttall says the French of Louisiana (?) call them, down the hill as far as I could see. Without moving, I looked about and saw its two eggs on the bare ground, on a slight shelf of the hill, on the dead pine-needles and sand, without any cavity or nest whatever, very obvious when once you had detected them, but not easily detected from their color, a coarse gray formed of white spotted with a bluish or slaty brown or umber,—a stone—granite—color, like the places it selects. I advanced and put my hand on them, and while I stooped, seeing a shadow on the ground, looked up and saw the bird, which had fluttered down the hill so blind and helpless, circling low and swiftly past over my head, showing the white spot on each wing in true nighthawk fashion. When I had gone a dozen rods, it appeared again higher in the air, with its peculiar fitting, limping kind of flight, all the while noiseless, and suddenly descending, it dashed at me within ten feet of my head, like an imp of darkness, then swept away high over the

pond, dashing now to this side now to that, on different tacks, as if, in pursuit of its prey, it had already forgotten its eggs on the earth. I can see how it might easily come to be regarded with superstitious awe.

June 7, 1853. Visited my nighthawk on her nest. Could hardly believe my eyes when I stood within seven feet and beheld her sitting on her eggs, her head to me. She looked so Saturnian, so one with the earth, so sphinx-like, a relic of the reign of Saturn which Jupiter did not destroy, a riddle that might well cause a man to go dash his head against a stone. It was not an actual living creature, far less a winged creature of the air, but a figure in stone or bronze, a fanciful production of art, like the gryphon or phoenix. In fact, with its breast toward me, and owing to its color or size no bill perceptible, it looked like the end [of] a brand, such as are common in a clearing, its breast mottled or alternately waved with dark brown and gray, its flat, grayish, weather-beaten crown, its eyes nearly closed, purposely, lest those bright beads should betray it, with the stony cunning of the sphinx. A fanciful work in bronze to ornament a mantel. It was enough to fill one with awe. The sight of this creature sitting on its eggs impressed me with the venerableness of the globe. There was nothing novel about it. All the while, this seemingly sleeping bronze sphinx, as motionless as the earth, was watching me with intense anxiety through those narrow slits in its eyelids. Another step, and it fluttered down the hill close to the ground, with a wabbling motion, as if touching the ground now with the tip of one wing, now with the other, so ten rods

to the water, which [it] skimmed close over a few rods, then rose and soared in the air above me. Wonderful creature, which sits motionless on its eggs on the barest, most exposed hills, through pelting storms of rain or hail, as if it were a rock or a part of the earth itself, the outside of the globe, with its eyes shut and its wings folded, and, after the two days' storm, when you think it has become a fit symbol of the rheumatism, it suddenly rises into the air a bird, one of the most aerial, supple, and graceful of creatures, without stiffness in its wings or joints! It was a fit prelude to meeting Prometheus bound to his rock on Caucasus.

June 8, 1853. As I stood by this pond, I heard a hawk scream, and, looking up, saw a pretty large one circling not far off and incessantly screaming, as I at first supposed to scare and so discover its prey, but its screaming was so incessant and it circled from time to time so near me, as I moved southward, that I began to think it had a nest near by and was angry at my intrusion into its domains. As I moved, the bird still followed and screamed, coming sometimes quite near or within gunshot, then circling far off or high into the sky. At length, as I was looking up at it, thinking it the only living creature within my view, I was singularly startled to behold, as my eye by chance penetrated deeper into the blue,—the abyss of blue above, which I had taken for a solitude,—its mate silently soaring at an immense height and seemingly indifferent to me. We are surprised to discover that there can be an eye on us on that side, and so little suspected, that the heavens are full of eyes, though they look so blue and spotless. Then I knew it was the female that circled and screamed below. At last the latter rose gradually to meet her mate, and they circled together there, as if they could not possibly feel any anxiety on my account. When I drew nearer to the tall trees where I suspected the nest to be, the female descended again, swept by screaming still nearer to me just over the tree-tops, and finally, while I was looking for the orchis in the swamp, alighted on a white pine twenty or thirty rods off. (The great

fringed orchis just open.) At length I detected the nest about eighty feet from the ground, in a very large white pine by the edge of the swamp. It was about three feet in diameter of dry sticks, and a young hawk, apparently as big as its mother, stood on the edge of the nest looking down at me, and only moving its head when I moved. In its imperfect plumage and by the slow motion of its head it reminded me strongly of a vulture, so large and gaunt. It appeared a tawny brown on its neck and breast, dark brown or blackish on wings. The mother was light beneath, and apparently lighter still on rump.

June 9, 1853. I have come with a spy-glass to look at the hawks. They have detected me and are already screaming over my head more than half a mile from the nest. I find no difficulty in looking at the young hawk (there appears to be one only, standing on the edge of the nest), resting the glass in the crotch of a young oak. I can see every wink and the color of its iris. It watches me more steadily than I it, now looking straight down at me with both eyes and outstretched neck, now turning its head and looking with one eye. How its eye and its whole head express anger! Its anger is more in its eye than in its beak. It is quite hoary over the eye and on the chin. The mother meanwhile is incessantly circling about and above its charge and me, farther or nearer, sometimes withdrawing a quarter of a mile, but occasionally coming to alight for a moment almost within gunshot, on the top of a tall white pine; but I hardly bring my glass fairly to bear on her, and get sight of her angry eye through the pine-needles, before she circles away again. Thus for an hour that I lay there, screaming every minute or oftener with open bill. Now and then pursued by a kingbird or a blackbird, who appear merely to annoy it by dashing down at its back. Meanwhile the male is soaring, apparently quite undisturbed, at a great height above, evidently not hunting, but amusing or recreating himself in the thinner and cooler air, as if pleased with his own circles, like a geometer, and enjoying the sublime scene. I doubt if he has his eye fixed on any prey, or the earth. He probably descends to hunt.

June 12, 1853. I forgot to say that I visited my hawk's nest, and the young hawk was perched now four or five feet above the nest, still in the shade. It will soon fly. Now, then, in secluded pine woods, the young hawks sit high on the edges of their nests or on the twigs near by in the shade, waiting for their pinions to grow, while their parents bring to them their prey. Their silence also is remarkable, not to betray themselves, nor will the old bird go to the nest while you are in sight. She pursues me half a mile when I withdraw.

June 13, 1853. 9 A.M. To Orchis Swamp. Find that there are two young hawks; one has left the nest and is perched on a small maple seven or eight rods distant. This one appears much smaller than the former one. I am struck by its large, naked head, so vulture-like, and large eyes, as if the vulture's were an inferior stage through which the

hawk passed. Its feet, too, are large, remarkably developed, by which it holds to its perch securely like an old bird, before its wings can perform their office. It has a buff breast, striped with dark brown. Pratt, when I told him of this nest, said he would like to carry one of his rifles down there. But I told him that I should be sorry to have them killed. I would rather save one of these hawks than have a hundred hens and chickens. It was worth more to see them soar, especially now that they are so rare in the landscape. It is easy to buy eggs, but not to buy hen-hawks. My neighbors would not hesitate to shoot the last pair of hen-hawks in the town to save a few of their chickens! But such economy is narrow and grovelling. It is unnecessarily to sacrifice the greater value to the less. I would rather never taste chickens' meat nor hens' eggs than never to see a hawk sailing through the upper air again. This sight is worth incomparably more than a chicken soup or a boiled egg. So we exterminate the deer and substitute the hog. It was amusing to observe the swaying to and fro of the young hawk's head to counterbalance the gentle motion of the bough in the wind.

June 16, 1853. Coming along near the celtis I heard a singular sound as of a bird in distress amid the bushes, and turned to relieve it. Next thought it a squirrel in an apple tree barking at me. Then found that it came from a hole in the ground under my feet, a loud sound between a grunting and a wheezing, yet not unlike the sound a red squirrel sometimes makes, but louder.

Looking down the hole, I saw the tail and hind quarters of a woodchuck, which seemed to be contending with another further down. Reaching down carefully, I took hold of the tail, and, though I had to pull very hard indeed, I drew him out between the rocks, a bounding great fat fellow, and tossed him a little way down the hill. As soon as he recovered from his bewilderment he made for the hole again, but, I barring the way, he ran off elsewhere.

June 17, 1853. One of the nighthawk's eggs is hatched. The young is unlike any that I have seen, exactly like a pinch of rabbit's fur or down of that color dropped on the ground, not two inches long, with a dimpling or geometrical or somewhat regular arrangement of minute feathers in the middle, destined to become the wings and tail. Yet even [then] it half opened its eye, and peeped if I mistake not. Was ever bird more completely protected, both by the color of eggs and of its own body that sits on them, and of the young bird just hatched? Accordingly the eggs and young are rarely discovered. There was one egg still, and by the side of it this little pinch of down, flattened out and not observed at first, and a foot down the hill had rolled a half of the egg it came out of. There was no callowness, as in the young of most birds. It seemed a singular place for a bird to begin its life,—to come out of its egg,—this little pinch of down,—and lie still on the exact spot where the egg lay, on a flat exposed shelf on the side of a bare hill, with nothing but the whole heavens, the broad universe above, to brood it when its mother was away.

June 18, 1853. Saturday. 4 A.M. By boat to Nawshawtuct; to Azalea Spring, or Pinxter Spring.

No fog and very little dew, or perhaps it was a slight rain in the night. I find always some dew in low ground. There is a broad crescent of clear sky in the west, but it looks rainy in the east. As yet we are disappointed of rain. Almost all birds appear to join the early morning chorus before sunrise on the roost, the matin hymn. I hear now the robin, the chip-bird, the blackbird, the martin, etc., etc., but I see none flying, or, at last, only one wing in the air, not yet illustrated by the sun.

As I was going up the hill, I was surprised to see rising above the June-grass, near a walnut, a whitish object, like a stone with a white top, or a skunk erect, for it was black below. It was an enormous toadstool, or fungus, a sharply conical parasol in the form of a sugar loaf, slightly turned up at the edges, which were rent half an inch in every inch or two. The whole height was sixteen inches. The pileus or cap was six inches long by seven in width at the rim, though it appeared longer than wide. There was no veil, and the stem was about one inch in diameter and naked. The top of the cap was quite white within and without. Hoariest at top of the cone

like a mountain-top, not smooth but with [a] stringy
kind of scales turned upward at the edge, which
declined downward, i.e. down the cap into a coarse
hoariness, as if the compact white fibres had been
burst by the spreading of the gills and showed the
black. As you looked up within, the light was
transmitted between the trembling gills. It looked
much like an old felt hat [that] is pushed up into a
cone and its rim all ragged and with some meal
shaken on to it; in fact, it was almost big enough
for a child's head. It was so delicate and fragile that
its whole cap trembled on the least touch, and, as
I could not lay it down without injuring it, I was
obliged to carry it home all the way in my hand.
It was a wonder how its soft cone ever broke
through the earth. Such growths ally our age to
former periods, such as geology reveals. I wondered
if it had not some relation to the skunk, though not
in odor, yet in its colors and the general impression
it made. It suggests a vegetative force which may
almost make man tremble for his dominion. It car-
ries me back to the era of the formation of the coal-
measures—the age of the saurus and pleiosaurus and
when bullfrogs were as big as bulls. Its stem had
something massy about it like an oak, large in proportion to the weight it had to support (though not
perhaps to the size of the cap), like the vast hollow
columns under some piazzas, whose caps have hardly weight enough to hold their tops together. It
made you think of parasols of Chinese mandarins;
or it might have been used by the great fossil
bullfrog in his walks. What part does it play in the
economy of the world?

I have just been out (7:30 A.M.) to show my

fungus. The milkman and the butcher followed me
to inquire what it was, and children and young
ladies addressed me in the street who never spoke
to me before. It is so fragile I was obliged to walk
at a funereal pace for fear of jarring it. It is so
delicately balanced on its stem that it falls to one
side across it on the least inclination; falls about like
an umbrella that has lost its stays. It is rapidly curl-
ing up on the edge, and the rents increasing, until

it is completely fringed, and is an inch wider there. It is melting in the sun and light, . . .black drops and streams falling on my hand and fragments of the black fringed rim falling on the sidewalk. Evidently such a plant can only be seen in perfection in the early morning. It is a creature of the night, like the great moths. They wish me to send it to the first of a series of exhibitions of flowers and fruits to be held at the court-house this afternoon, which I promise to do if it is presentable then. Perhaps it might be placed in the court-house cellar and the company be invited at last to walk down and examine it. Think of placing this giant parasol fungus in the midst of all their roses; yet they admit that it would overshadow and eclipse them all. It is to be remarked that this grew, not in low and damp soil, but high up on the open side of a dry hill, about two rods from a walnut and one from a wall, in the midst of a rising above the thin June-grass. The last night was warm; the earth was very dry; and there was a slight sprinkling of rain.

June 20, 1853. Saw a little skunk coming up the river-bank in the woods at the White Oak, a funny little fellow, about six inches long and nearly as broad. It faced me and actually compelled me to retreat before it for five minutes. Perhaps I was between it and its hole. Its broad black tail, tipped with white, was erect like a kitten's. It had what looked like a broad white band drawn tight across its forehead or top-head, from which two lines of white ran down, one on each side of its back, and there was a narrow white line down its snout. It raised its back, sometimes ran a few feet forward, sometimes backward, and repeatedly turned its tail to me, prepared to discharge its fluid like the old. Such was its instinct. And all the while it kept up a fine grunting like a little pig or a squirrel. It reminded me that the red squirrel, the woodchuck, and the skunk all made a similar sound. Now there are young rabbits, skunks, and probably woodchucks.

March 10, 1854. Saw a skunk in the Corner road, which I followed sixty rods or more. Out now about 4 P.M.,—partly because it is a dark, foul day. It is a slender black (and white) animal, with its back remarkably arched, standing high behind and carrying its head low; runs, even when undisturbed, with a singular teeter or undulation, like the walking of a Chinese lady. Very slow; I hardly have to run to keep up with it. It has a long tail, which regularly erects when I come too near and prepares to discharge its liquid. It is white at the end of the tail, and the hind head and a line on the front of the face,—the rest black, except the flesh-colored nose (and I think feet). The back is more arched and the fore and hind feet nearer together in my sketch. It tried repeatedly to get into the wall, and did not show much cunning. Finally it steered, apparently, for an old skunk or woodchuck hole under a wall four rods off, and got into it,—or under the wall, at least,—for it was stopped up,—and there I view at leisure close to. It has a remarkably long, narrow, pointed head and snout, which enable it to make those deep narrow holes in the earth by which it probes for insects. Its eyes have an innocent, childlike, bluish-black expression. It made a singular loud patting sound repeatedly, on the frozen ground under the wall, undoubtedly with its fore feet (I saw only the upper part of the animal), which reminded me of what I have heard about your stopping and stamping in order to stop the skunk. Probably it has to do with its getting its food,—patting the earth to get the insects or worms. Though why it did so then I know not.

Its track was small, round, showing the nails, a little less than an inch in diameter, alternate five or six inches by two or two and a half, sometimes two feet together. There is something pathetic in such a sight,—next to seeing one of the human aborigines of the country. I respect the skunk as a human being in a very humble sphere. I have no doubt they have begun to probe already where the ground permits,—or as far as it does. But what have they eat all winter?

March 21, 1854. Tuesday. At sunrise to Clamshell Hill. River skimmed over at Willow Bay last night. Thought I should find ducks cornered up by the ice; they get behind this hill for shelter. Saw what looked like clods of plowed meadow rising above the ice. Looked with glass and found it to be more than thirty black ducks asleep with their heads in [*sic*] their backs, motionless, and thin ice formed about them. Soon one or two were moving about slowly. There was an open space, eight or ten rods by one or two. At first all within a space of apparently less than a rod [in] diameter. It was 6:30 A.M., and the sun shining on them, but bitter cold. How tough they are! I crawled far on my stomach and got a near view of them, thirty rods off. At length they detected me and quacked. Some got out upon the ice, and when I rose up all took to flight in a great straggling flock which at a distance looked like crows, in no order. Yet when you see two or three, the parallelism produced by their necks and bodies steering the same way gives the idea of order.

A *pril 8, 1854.* At Nut Meadow Brook saw, or rather heard, a muskrat plunge into the brook before me, and saw him endeavoring in vain to bury himself in the sandy bottom, looking like an amphibious animal. I stooped and, taking him by his tail, which projected, tossed him ashore. He did not lose the points of compass, but turned directly to the brook again, though it was toward me, and plunging in, buried himself in the mud, and that was the last I saw of him.

M *ay 8, 1854.* I saw, in the Miles meadow, on the bottom, two painted tortoises fighting. Their sternums were not particularly depressed. The

smaller had got firmly hold of the loose skin of the larger's neck with his jaws, and most of the time his head was held within the other's shell; but, though he thus had the "upper hand," he had the least command of himself and was on his edge. They were very moderate,—for the most part quite still, as if weary,—and were not to be scared by me. Then they struggled a little, their flippers merely paddling the water, and I could hear the edges of their shells strike together. I took them out into the boat, holding by the smaller, which did not let go of the larger, and so raising both together. Nor did he let go when they were laid in the boat. But when I put them into the water again they instantly separated and concealed themselves.

May 16, 1854. On Hubbard's meadow, saw a motion in the water as if a pickerel had darted away; approached and saw a middle-sized snapping turtle on the bottom; managed at last, after stripping off my coat and rolling up my shirt-sleeve, by thrusting in my arm to the shoulder, to get him by the tail and lift him aboard. He tried to get under the boat. He snapped at my shoe and got the toe in his mouth. His back was covered with green moss (?), or the like, mostly concealing the scales. In this were small leeches. Great, rough, but not hard, scales on his legs. He made a pretty loud hissing like a cross dog, by his breathing. It was wonderful how suddenly this sluggish creature would snap at anything. As he lay under the seat, I scratched his back, and, filling himself with air and rage, his head would suddenly fly upward, his shell striking the seat, just as a steel trap goes off, and though I was prepared for it, it never failed to startle me, it was so swift and sudden. He slowly inflated himself, and then suddenly went off like a percussion lock snapping in the air. Thus undoubtedly he catches fishes, as a toad catches flies. His laminated tail and great triangular points in the rear edge of his shell. Nature does not forget beauty of outline even in a mud turtle's shell.

May 17, 1854. 5:30 A.M. To Island. The water is now tepid in the morning to the hands (may have been a day or two), as I slip my hands down the paddle. Hear the wood pewee, the warm-weather sound. As I was returning over the meadow this side of the Island, I saw the snout of a mud turtle above the surface,—little more than an inch of the point,—and paddled toward it. Then, as he moved slowly on the surface, different parts of his shell and head just appearing looked just like the scalloped edges of some pads which had just reached the surface. I pushed up and found a large snapping turtle on the bottom. He appeared of a dirty brown there, very nearly the color of the bottom at present. With his great head, as big as an infant's, and his vigilant eyes as he paddled about on the bottom in his attempts to escape, he looked not merely repulsive, but to some extent terrible even as a crocodile. At length, after thrusting my arm in up to the shoulder two or three times, I succeeded in getting him into the boat, where I secured him with a lever under a seat. I could get him from the landing to the house only by turning him over and drawing him by the tail, the hard crests of which afforded a good hold; for he was so heavy that I

could not hold him off so far as to prevent his snapping at my legs. He weighed thirty and a half
pounds.

Extreme length of shell . . . . 15 ½ inches
Length of shell in middle 15   ”
Greatest width of shell . . . . 12 ½   ”
(This was toward the rear.)
Tail (beyond shell) . . . . 11 ½   ”

His head and neck it was not easy to measure,
but, judging from the proportions of one described
by [D.H.] Storer, they must have been 10 inches
long at least, which makes the whole length 37 inches. Width of head 4 ½ inches; with the skin of the
neck, more than 5. His sternum, which was slightly depressed, was 10 ½ by 5 ½. Depth from back
to sternum about 7 inches. There were six great
scallops, or rather triangular points, on the hind
edge of his shell, three on each side, the middle one
of each three the longest, about ¾ of an inch. He
had surprisingly stout hooked jaws, of a gray color
or bluish-gray, the upper shutting over the under,
a more or less sharp triangular beak corresponding
to one below; and his flippers were armed with very
stout claws 1 ¼ inches long. He had a very ugly and
spiteful face (with a vigilant gray eye, which was
never shut in any position of the head), surrounded by the thick and ample folds of the skin about
his neck. His shell was comparatively smooth and
free from moss,—a dirty black. He was a *dirty* or
speckled white beneath. He made the most
remarkable and awkward appearance when walking. The edge of his shell was lifted about eight inches from the ground, tilting now to this side, then

to that, his great scaly legs or flippers hanging with flesh and loose skin, — slowly and gravely (?) hissing the while. His walking was perfectly elephantine. Thus he stalked along,—a low conical mountain,—dragging his tail, with his head turned upward with the ugliest and most venomous look, on his flippers, half leg half fin. But he did not proceed far before he sank down to rest. If he could support a world on his back when lying down, he certainly could not stand up under it. All said that he walked like an elephant. When lying on his back, showing his *dirty* white and warty under side, with his tail curved round, he reminded you forcibly of pictures of the dragon. He could not easily turn himself back; tried many times in vain, resting betweenwhiles. Would inflate himself and convulsively spring with head and all upward, so as to lift his shell from the ground, and he would strike his head on the ground, lift up his shell, and catch at the earth with his claws. His back was of two great blunt ridges with a hollow between, down the middle of which was a slight but distinct ridge also. There was also a ridge of spines more or less hard on each side of his crested tail. Some of these spines in the crest of the tail were nearly half an inch high. Storer says that they have five *claws* on the fore legs, but only four on the hind ones. In this there was a *perfectly* distinct fifth toe (?) on the hind legs, though it did not pierce the skin; and on the fore legs it did not much more. S. does not say how many toes he has. These claws must be powerful to dig with.

This, then, is the season for hunting them, now that the water is warmer, before the pads are common, and the water is getting shallow on the meadows. E[lijah] Wood, Senior, speaks of two seen fighting for a long time in the river in front of his house last year. I have heard of one being found in the meadow in the winter surrounded by frozen mud. Is not this the heaviest animal found wild in this township? Certainly none but the otter approaches it. Farrar says that, when he was eleven, one which he could not lift into the boat towed him across the river; weighed twenty-nine [pounds]. . .

The turtle was very sluggish, though capable of putting forth great strength. He would just squeeze into a flour barrel and would not quite lie flat in it when his head and tail were drawn in. There was [a] triangular place in the bottom of his mouth and an orifice within it through which, apparently, he breathed, the orifice opening and shutting. I hear of a man who injured his back seriously for many years by carrying one some distance at arm's length to prevent his biting him. They are frequently seen fighting and their shells heard striking together.

*J*__*une 7, 1854.*__ P.M. To Dugan Desert *via* Linnæa Hills. As I expected I find the desert scored by the tracks of turtles, made evidently last night, though the rain of this morning has obliterated the marks of their tails. The tracks are about seven eights of an inch in diameter, one half inch deep, two inches apart (from centre to centre) in each row, and the rows four or five inches apart; and they have dabbled in the sand in many places and made some small holes. Yesterday was hot and dusty, and this morning it rained. Did they choose such a time? Yesterday I saw the painted and the wood tortoise out. Now I see a snapping turtle, its shell about a foot long, out here on the damp sand, with its head out, disturbed by me. It had just been excavating, and its shell—especially the fore part and sides—and especially its snout, were deeply covered with earth. It appears to use its shell as a kind of spade whose handle is within, tilting it now this way, now that, and perhaps using its head and claws as a pick. It was in a little cloud of mosquitoes, which were continually settling on its head and flippers, but which it did not mind. Its sternum was slightly depressed. It seems that they are very frequently found fighting in the water and sometimes dead in the spring, maybe killed by the ice. Some think that the suckers I see floating are killed by the ice.

June 15, 1854. 5:30 A.M. To Island and Hill. A young painted tortoise on the surface of the water, as big as a quarter of a dollar, with a reddish or orange sternum. I suppose that my skater insect is the hydrometer. Found a nest of tortoise eggs, apparently buried last night, which I brought home, ten in all,—one lying wholly on the surface,—and buried in the garden. The soil *above* a dark virgin mould about a stump was unexpectedly hard.

June 18, 1854. I discover that J. Dugan found the eggs of my snapping turtle of June 7th, apparently the same day. It did not go to a new place then, after all. I opened the nest to-day. It is, perhaps, five or six rods from the brook, in the sand near its edge. The surface had been disturbed over a foot and a half in diameter and was *slightly* concave. The nest commenced five inches beneath, and at its neck was two and a half inches across and from this nearly four inches deep, and swelled out below to four inches in width; shaped like a short, rounded bottle with a broad mouth; and the surrounding sand was quite firm. I took out forty-two eggs, close packed, and Dugan says he had previously broken one, which made forty-three. (Daniel Foster says he found forty-two this summer, in a nest in his field in Princeton.) They are a dirty white and spherical, a little more than one and one sixteenth inches in diameter,—softshelled, so that my finger left a permanent dimple in them. It was now ten days since they had been laid, and a little more than one half of each was darker-colored (probably the lower half) and the other white and dry-looking. I opened one, but could detect no organization with the unarmed eye. The halves of the shell, as soon as emptied, curled up, as we see them where the skunks have sucked them. They must all have been laid at one time. If it were not for the skunks, and probably other animals, we should be overrun with them. Who can tell how many tortoise eggs are buried thus in this small desert?

June 21, 1854. In the little meadow pool, or bay, in Hubbard's shore, I see two old pouts tending their countless young close to the shore. The former are slate-colored. The latter are about half an inch long and very black, forming a dark mass from eight to twelve inches in diameter. The old are constantly circling around them,—over and under and *through*,—as if anxiously endeavoring to keep them together, from time to time moving off five or six feet to reconnoitre. The whole mass of

the young—and there must be a thousand of them at least—is incessantly moving, pushing forward and stretching out. Are often in the form of a great pout, apparently keeping together by their own instinct chiefly, now on the bottom, now rising to the top. Alone they might be mistaken for pollywogs. The old, at any rate, do not appear to be very successful in their apparent efforts to communicate with and direct them. At length they break into four parts. The old are evidently very careful parents. One has some wounds apparently. In the second part of the story of Tanner it is said: "*Ah-wa-sis-sie*—Little catfish. The Indians say this fish hatches its young in a hole in the mud, and that they accompany her for some time afterwards." Yet in Ware's Smellie it is said that fishes take no care of their young. I think also that I see the young breams in schools hovering over their nests while the old are still protecting them.

July 10, 1854. Monday. Took up one of the small tortoise eggs which I had buried June 15th. The eye was remarkable, developed in the colorless and almost formless head, one or two large dark circles of the full diameter; a very distinct pulsation where the heart should be and along the neck was perceptible; but there seemed to be no body but a mass of yellow yolk.

July 30, 1854. Opened one of the snapping turtle's eggs at Dugan Desert, laid June 7th. There is a little mud turtle squirming in it, apparently perfect in outline, shell and all, but all *soft* and of one consistency,—a bluish white, with a mass of yellowish yolk (?) attached. Perhaps it will be [a] month more before it is hatched.

August 26, 1854. Opened one of my snapping turtle's eggs. The egg was not warm to the touch. The young is now larger and darker-colored, shell and all, more than a hemisphere, and the yolk which maintains it is much reduced. Its shell, very deep, hemispherical, fitting close to the shell of the egg, and, if you had not just opened the egg, you would say it could not contain so much. Its shell is considerably hardened, its feet and claws developed, and also its great head, though held in for want of room. Its eyes are open. It puts out its head, stretches forth its claws, and liberates its tail, though all were enveloped in a gelatinous fluid. With its great head it has already the ugliness of the full-grown, and is already a hieroglyphic of snappishness. It may take a fortnight longer to hatch it.

How much lies quietly buried in the ground that we wot not of! We unconsciously step over the eggs of snapping turtles slowly hatching the summer through. Not only was the surface perfectly dry and trackless there, but blackberry vines had run over the spot where these eggs were buried and

weeds had sprung up above. If Iliads are not composed in our day, snapping turtles are hatched and
arrive at maturity. It already thrusts forth its tremen-
dous head,—for the first time in this sphere,—and
slowly moves from side to side,—opening its small
glistening eyes for the first time to the light,—
expressive of dull rage, as if it had endured the trials
of this world for a century. When I behold this
monster thus steadily advancing toward maturity,
all nature abetting, I am convinced that there must
be an irresistable necessity for mud turtles. With
what tenacity nature sticks to her idea! These eggs,
not warm to the touch, buried in the ground, so
slow to hatch are like the seeds of vegetable life.

September 2, 1954. Opened one of my snapping turtle's eggs. The young alive, but not very
lively, with shell dark grayishblack; yolk as big as
a hazelnut; tail curled round and is considerably
longer than the shell, and slender; three ridges on
back, one at edges of plates on each side of dorsal,
which is very prominent. There is only the trace of
a dorsal ridge in the old. Eye open. . .

To my great surprise I find this morning
(September 3d) that the little unhatched turtle,
which I thought was sickly and dying, and left out
on the grass in the rain yesterday morn, thinking
it would be quite dead in a few minutes—I find the
[egg] shell alone and the turtle a foot or two off
vigorously crawling, with neck outstretched
(holding up its head and looking round like an old
one) and feet surmounting every obstacle. It climbs
up the nearly perpendicular side of a basket with
the yolk attached. They thus not only continue to

live after they are dead, but begin to live before they are alive!

September 4, 1854. I have provided my little snapping turtle with a tub of water and mud, and it is surprising how fast he learns to use his limbs and this world. He actually runs, with the yolk still trailing from him, as if he had got new vigor from the contact with the mud. The insensibility and toughness of his infancy make our life, with its disease and low spirits, ridiculous. He impresses me as the rudiment of a man worthy to inhabit the earth. He is born with a shell. That is symbolical of his toughness. His shell being so rounded and sharp on the back at this age, he can turn over without trouble.

September 9, 1954. This morning I find a little hole, three quarters of an inch or an inch over, above my small tortoise eggs, and find a young tortoise coming out (apparently in the rainy night) just beneath. It is the *Sternothærus odoratus*—already has the strong scent—and now has drawn in its head and legs. I see no traces of the yolk, or what-not, attached. It may have been out of the egg some days. *Only one* as yet. I buried them in the garden June 15th.

I am affected by the thought that the earth nurses these eggs. They are planted in the earth, and the earth takes care of them; she is genial to them and does not kill them. It suggests a certain vitality and intelligence in the earth, which I had not realized. This mother is not merely inanimate and inorganic. Though the immediate mother turtle abandons her offspring, the earth and sun are kind to

them. The old turtle on which the earth rests takes care of them while the other waddles off. Earth was not made poisonous and deadly to them. The earth has some virtue in it; when seeds are put into it, they germinate; when turtles' eggs, they hatch in due time. Though the mother turtle remained and brooded them, it would still nevertheless be the universal world turtle which, through her, cared for them as now. Thus the earth is the mother of all creatures.

Garfield said that one of his sons, while they were haying in the river meadows once, found a hundred little pickerel, an inch or inch and a half long, in [a] little hole in the meadow not bigger than a bushel basket and nearly dry. He took them out and put them into the river. Another time he himself found many hundreds in a ditch, brought them home, and put them into his large tub. There they lived a spell without his feeding them, but, small as they were, lived on one another, and you could see the tails sticking out their mouths. It would seem as if their spawn was deposited in those little muddy-bottomed hollows in the meadows where we find the schools of young thus landlocked.

*S*eptember 11, 1854. Measured to-day the little *Sternothærus odoratus* which came out the ground in the garden September 9th. Its shell is thirty-two fortieths of an inch long, by twenty-five fortieths wide. It has a distinct dorsal ridge, and its head and flippers are remarkably developed. Its raised back and dorsal ridge, as in the case of the mud turtle, enable it to turn over very easily. It may have been hatched some time before it came out, for not only was there no trace of the *yolk (?)*, but its shell was much wider than the egg, when it first came out of the ground. I placed a sieve over it, and it remained in the hole it had made mostly concealed the two rainy days,—the 9th and 10th,—but to-day I found it against the edge of the sieve, its head and legs drawn in and quite motionless, so that you would have said the pulses of life had not fairly begun to beat. I put it into the tub on the edge of the mud. It seems that it does not have to learn to walk, but walks at once. It seems to have no infancy such as birds have. It is surprising how much cunning it already exhibits. It is defended both by its form and color and its instincts. As it lay on the mud, its color made it very inobvious, but, besides, it kept its head and legs drawn in and perfectly still, as if feigning death; but this was not sluggishness. At a little distance I watched it for ten minutes or more.

At length it put its head out far enough to see if the coast was clear, then, with its flippers, it turned itself toward the water (which element it had never seen before), and suddenly and with rapidity launched itself into it and dove to the bottom. Its whole behavior was calculated to enable it to reach its proper element safely and without attracting attention. Not only was it made of a color and form (like a bit of coal) which alone almost effectually concealed it, but it was made, infant as it was, to be perfectly still as if inanimate and then to move with rapidity when unobserved. The oldest turtle does not show more, if so much cunning. I think I may truly say that it uses its cunning and meditates how it may reach the water in safety. When I first took it out of its hole on the morning of the 9th, it shrunk into its shell and was motionless, feigning death. That this was not sluggishness, I have proved. When to-day it lay within half an inch of the water's edge, it knew it for a friendly element and, without deliberation or experiment, but at last when it thought me and all foes unobservant of its motions, with remarkable precipitation it committed itself to it as if realizing a longcherished idea. Plainly all its motions were as much the result of what is called instinct as is the act of sucking in infants. Our own subtlest [sic] is likewise but another kind of instinct. The wise man is a wise infant obeying his finest and neverfailing instincts. It does not so much impress me as an infantile beginning of life as an epitome of all the past of turtledom and of the earth. I think of it as the result of all the turtles that have been.

The little snapping turtle lies almost constantly on the mud with its snout out of water. It does not keep under water long. Yesterday in the cold rain, however, it lay buried in the mud all day!

September 16, 1854. I find the mud turtle's eggs at the Desert all hatched. There is a small hole by which they have made their exit some time before the last rain (of the 14th) and since I was here on the 4th. There is, however, one still left in the nest. As the eggs were laid the 7th of June, it makes about three months before they came out of the ground. The nest was full of sand and eggshells. I saw no tracks of the old one. I took out the remaining one, which perhaps could not get out alone, and it began slowly to crawl toward the brook about five rods distant. It went about five feet in as many minutes. At this rate it would have reached the water in a couple of hours at most. Then, being disturbed by my moving, stopped, and, when it started again, retraced its steps, crossed the hole which I had filled, and got into a rut leading toward another part of the brook, about ten rods distant. It climbed directly over some weeds and tufts of grass in its way. Now and then it paused, stretched out its head, looked round, and appeared to be deliberating, waiting for information or listening to its instinct. It seemed to be but a blundering instinct which it obeyed and as if it might be easily turned from its proper course. Yet in no case did it go wholly wrong. Whenever I took it up, it drew in its head and legs, shut its eyes, and remained motionless. It was so slow that I could not stop to watch it, and so carried it to within seven or eight inches of the water, turning its head inland. At length it put out its head and legs, turned itself round, crawled to the water, and endeavored as soon as it entered it to bury itself at the bottom, but, it being sand, it could not. I put it further into the stream, and it was at once carried down head over heels by the current. I think they come out in the night.

Another little sternothærus has come out of the ground since eight this morning (it is now 11 A.M.). (Another, Sept. 17th, found in morning. Another the 18th, between 8 and 11 A.M. Another the 18th, between 11 A.M. and 1 P.M. Another between 1 and 3 P.M. the 18th. Another found out on the morning of the 19th. Another was dug out the 25th. All hatched, then, but one egg which I have. A snapping turtle had come out on the morning of the 20th, one at least. Another on the morning of the 23d Sept. Another on the morning of the 26th.) The first sternothærus has remained buried in the mud in the tub from the first, and the snapping turtle also for the last few days.

January 31, 1855. As I skated near the shore under Lee's Cliff, I saw what I took to be some scrags or knotty stubs of a dead limb lying on the bank beneath a white oak, close by me. Yet while I looked directly at them I could not but admire their close resemblance to partridges. I had come along with a rapid whir and suddenly halted right against them, only two rods distant, and, as my eyes watered a little from skating against the wind, I was not convinced that they were birds till I had pulled out my glass and deliberately examined them. They sat and stood, three of them, perfectly still with their heads erect, some darker feathers like ears, methinks, increasing their resemblance to scrabs [*sic*], as where a small limb is broken off. I was much surprised at the remarkable stillness they preserved, instinctively relying on the resemblance to the ground for their protection, *i.e.* withered grass, dry oak leaves, dead scrags, and broken twigs. I thought at first that it was a dead oak limb with a few stub ends or scrabbs [*sic*] sticking up, and for some time after I had noted the resemblance to birds, standing only two rods off, I could not be sure of their character on account of their perfect motionlessness, and it was not till I brought my glass to bear on them and saw their eyes distinctly, steadily glaring on me, their necks and every muscle tense with anxiety, that I was convinced. At length, on some signal which I did not perceive, they went with a whir, as if shot, off over the bushes.

March 22, 1855. Going [along] the steep side-hill on the south of [Fair Haven] Pond about 4 P.M., on the edge of the little patch of wood which the choppers have not yet levelled,—though they have felled many an acre around it this winter,—I observed a rotten and hollow hemlock stump about two feet high and six inches in diameter, and instinctively approached with my right hand ready to cover it. I found a flying squirrel in it, which, as my left hand had covered a small hole at the bottom, ran directly into my right hand. It struggled and bit not a little, but my cotton glove protected me, and I felt its teeth only once or twice. It also uttered three or four dry shrieks at first, something like *cr-r-rack cr-r-r-ack cr-r-r-ack*. I rolled it up in my handkerchief and, holding the ends tight, carried it home in my hand, some three miles. It struggled more or less all the way, especially when my feet made any unusual or louder noise going through leaves or bushes. I could count its claws as they appeared through the handkerchief, and once it got its head out a hole. It even bit through the handkerchief.

Color, as I remember, above a chestnut ash, inclining to fawn or cream color (?), slightly browned; beneath white, the under edge of its wings (?) tinged yellow, the upper dark, perhaps black, making a dark stripe. [John James] Audubon and [John] Bachman do not speak of any such stripe! It was a very cunning little animal, reminding me of a mouse in the room. Its very large and prominent black eyes gave it an interesting innocent look. Its very neat flat, fawn-colored, distichous tail was a great ornament. Its "sails" were not very obvious when it was at rest, merely giving it a flat appearance beneath. It would leap off and upward into the air two or three feet from a table, spreading its "sails," and fall to the floor in vain; perhaps strike the side of the room in its upward spring and endeavor to cling to it. It would run up the window by the sash, but evidently found the furniture and walls and floor too hard and smooth for it and after some falls became quiet. In a few moments it allowed me to stroke it, though far from confident.

I put it in a barrel and covered it for the night. It was quite busy all the evening gnawing out, clinging for this purpose and gnawing at the upper edge of a sound oak barrel, and then dropping to rest from time to time. It had defaced the barrel considerably by morning, and would probably have escaped if I had not placed a piece of iron against the gnawed part. I had left in the barrel some bread, apple, shagbarks, and cheese. It ate some of the apple and one shagbark, cutting it quite in two transversely.

In the morning it was quiet, and *squatted* somewhat curled up amid the straw, with its tail passing under it and the end curled over its head very prettily, as if to shield it from the light and keep it warm. I always found it in this position by day when I raised the lid.

March 23, 1855. P.M. To Fair Haven Pond. Carried my flying squirrel back to the woods in my handkerchief. I placed it, about 3:30 P.M., on the very stump I had taken it from. It immediately ran about a rod over the leaves and up a slender maple sapling about ten feet, then after a moment's pause sprang off and skimmed downward toward a large maple nine feet distant, whose trunk it struck three or four feet from the ground. Thus it rapidly ascended, on the opposite side from me, nearly thirty feet, and there clung to the main stem with its head downward, eyeing me. After two or three minutes' pause I saw that it was preparing for another spring by raising its head and looking off, and away it went in admirable style, more like a bird than any quadruped I had dreamed of and far surpassing the impression I had received from naturalists' accounts. I marked the spot it started from and the place where it struck, and measured the height and distance carefully. It sprang off from the maple at the height of twenty-eight and a half feet, and struck the ground at the foot of a tree fifty and a half feet distant, measured horizontally. Its

flight was not a *regular* descent; it varied from a
direct line both horizontally and vertically.

Indeed it skimmed much like a hawk and part
of its flight was nearly horizontal, and it diverged
from a right line eight or ten feet to the right, making a curve in that direction. There were six trees
from six inches to a foot in diameter, one a hemlock,
in a direct line between the two termini, and these
it skimmed partly round, and passed through their

thinner limbs; did not as I could perceive touch a twig. It skimmed its way like a hawk between and around the trees. Though it was a windy day, this was on a steep hillside away from the wind and covered with wood, so it was not aided by that. As the ground rose about two feet, the distance was to the absolute height as fifty and a half to twenty-six and a half, or it advanced about two feet for every one foot of descent. After its vain attempts in the house, I was not prepared for this exhibition. It did not fall heavily as in the house, but struck the ground gently enough, and I cannot believe that the mere extension of the skin enabled it to skim so far. It must be still further aided by its organization. Perhaps it fills itself with air first. Perhaps I had a fairer view than common of its flight, now at 3:30 P.M. Audubon and Bachman say *he* saw it skim "about fifty yards," curving upwards at the end and alighting on the trunk of a tree. This in a meadow in which were scattered oaks and beeches. This near Philadelphia. Wesson [?] says he has seen them fly five or six rods.

Kicking over the hemlock stump, which was a mere shell with holes below, and a poor refuge, I was surprised to find a little nest at the bottom, open above just like a bird's nest, a mere bed. It was composed of leaves, shreds of bark, and dead pine-needles. As I remember, it was not more than an inch and a half broad when at rest, but when skimming through the air I should say it was four inches broad. This is the impression I now have. Captain John Smith says it is said to fly thirty or forty yards. Audubon and Bachman quote one Gideon B. Smith, M.D., of Baltimore, who has had much to do with these squirrels and speaks of their curving upward at the end of their flight to alight on a treetrunk and of their "flying" into his windows. In order to perform all these flights,—to strike a tree at such a distance, etc., etc.,— it is evident it must be able to steer. I should say that mine steered as a hawk that moves without flapping its wings, never being able, however, to get a new impetus after the first spring.

May 7, 1855. Climbed a hemlock to a very large and complete, probably gray squirrel's, nest, eighteen inches [in] diameter,—a foundation of twigs, on which a body of leaves and some bark fibres, lined with the last, and the whole covered with many fresh green hemlock twigs one foot or more long with the leaves on,—which had been gnawed off,—and many strewed the ground beneath, having fallen off. Entrance one side.

A short distance beyond this and the hawk's-nest pine, I observed a middling-sized red oak standing a little aslant on the sidehill over the swamp,

with a pretty large hole in one side about fifteen feet from the ground, where apparently a limb on which a felled tree lodged had been cut some years before and so broke out a cavity. I thought that such a hole was too good a one not to be improved by some inhabitant of the wood. Perhaps the gray squirrels I had just seen had their nest there. Or was not the entrance big enough to admit a screech owl? So I thought I would tap on it and put my ear to the trunk and see if I could hear anything stirring within it, but I heard nothing. Then I concluded to look into it. So I shinned up, and when I reached up one hand to the hole to pull myself up by it, the thought passed through my mind perhaps something may take hold of my fingers, but nothing did. The first limb was nearly opposite to the hole, and, resting on this, I looked in, and, to my great surprise, there squatted, filling the hole, which was about six inches deep and five to six wide, a salmon-brown bird not so long as a partridge, seemingly asleep within three inches of the top and close to my face. It was a minute or two before I made it out to be an owl. It was a salmon-brown or fawn (?) above, the feathers shafted with small blackish-brown somewhat hastate (?) marks, *grayish* toward the ends of the wings and tail, as far as I could see. A large white circular space about or behind eye, banded in rear by a pretty broad (one third of an inch) and quite conspicuous perpendicular *dark*-brown stripe. Egret, say one and a quarter inches long, sharp, triangular, reddishbrown without mainly. It lay crowded in that small space, with its tail somewhat bent up and one side of its head turned up with one egret, and its large dark eye open only by a long slit about a sixteenth of an inch wide; visible breathing. After a little while I put in one hand and stroked it repeatedly, whereupon it reclined its head a little lower and closed its eye entirely. Though

curious to know what was under it, I disturbed it
no farther at that time.

In the meanwhile, the crows were making a
great cawing amid and over the pine-tops beyond
the swamp, and at intervals I heard the screams of
a hawk, probably the surviving male hen-hawk,
whom they were pestering (unless they had
discovered the male screech owl), and a part of them
came cawing about me. This was a very fit place for
hawks and owls to dwell in,—the thick woods just
over a white spruce swamp, in which the glaucous
kalmia grows; the gray squirrels, partridges, hawks,
and owls, all together. It was probably these screech
owls which I heard in moonlight nights hereabouts
last fall. . .

Returning by owl's nest about one hour before
sunset, I climbed up and looked in again. The owl
was gone, but there were four nearly round *dirty
brownish white* eggs, quite warm, on nothing but
the bits of rotten wood which made the bottom of

the hole. The eggs were very nearly as large at one end as the other, slightly oblong, 1⅜ inches by 1⅞, as nearly as I could measure. I took out one. It would probably have hatched within a week, the young being considerably feathered and the bill remarkably developed. Perhaps she heard me coming, and so left the nest. My bird corresponds in color, as far as I saw it, with Wilson's *Strix asio*, but not his nævia, which Nuttall and others consider a young (?) bird, though the egg was not pure white. I do not remember that my bird was barred or *mottled* at all.

May 12, 1855. As I approached the owl's nest, I saw her run past the hole up into that part of the hollow above it, and probably she was there when I thought she had flown on the 7th. I looked in, and at first did not know what I saw. One of the three remaining eggs was hatched, and a little downy *white* young one, two or three times as long as an egg, lay helpless between the two remaining eggs. Also a dead white-bellied mouse (*Mus leucopus*) lay with them, its tail curled round one of the eggs. Wilson says of his red owl (*Strix asio*),—with which this apparently corresponds, and not with the mottled, though my egg is not "pure white,"—that "the young are at first covered with a whitish down."

June 2, 1855. Still windier than before, and yet no rain. It is now very dry indeed, and the grass is suffering. Some springs commonly full at this season are dried up. The wind shakes the house night and day. From that cocoon of the *Attacus cecropia* which I found—I think it was on the 24th of May—on a red maple shrub, three or four feet from the ground, on the edge of the meadow by the new Bedford road just this side of Beck Stow's, came out this forenoon a splendid moth. I had pinned the cocoon to the sash at the upper part of my window and quite forgotten it. About the middle of the forenoon Sophia [Thoreau's sister] came in

and exclaimed that there was a moth on my window. At first I supposed that she meant a cloth-eating moth, but it turned out that my *A. cecropia* had come out and dropped down to the window-sill, where it hung on the *side* of a slipper (which was inserted into another) to let its wings hang down and develop themselves. At first the wings were not only not unfolded laterally, but not longitudinally, the thinner ends of the forward ones for perhaps three quarters of an inch being very feeble and occupying very little space. It was surprising to see the creature unfold and expand before our eyes, the wings gradually elongating, as it were by their own gravity; and from time to time the insect assisted this operation by a slight shake. It was wonderful how it waxed and grew, revealing some new beauty every fifteen minutes, which I called Sophia to see, but never losing its hold on the shoe. It looked like a young emperor just donning the most splendid ermine robes that ever emperor wore, the wings every moment acquiring greater expansion and their

at first wrinkled edge becoming more tense. At first
its wings appeared double, one within another. At
last it advanced so far as to spread its wings completely but feebly when we approached. This occupied several hours. It continued to hang to the
shoe, with its wings ordinarily closed erect behind
its back, the rest of the day; and at dusk, when apparently it was waving its wings preparatory to its
evening flight, I gave it ether and so saved it in a
perfect state. As it lies, not spread to the utmost, it
is five and nine tenths inches by two and a quarter.

June 18, 1855. To Hemlocks. At 3 P.M., as I
walked up the bank by the Hemlocks, I saw a
painted tortoise just beginning its hole; then
another a dozen rods from the river on the bare
barren field near some pitch pines, where the earth
was covered with cladonias, cinquefoil, sorrel, etc.
Its hole was about two thirds done. I stooped down
over it, and, to my surprise, after a slight pause it
proceded in its work, directly under and within
eighteen inches of my face. I retained a constrained
position for three quarters of an hour or more for
fear of alarming it. It rested on its fore legs, the front
part of its shell about one inch higher than the
rear, and this position was not changed essentially
to the last. The hole was oval, broadest behind,
about one inch wide and one and three quarters
long, and the dirt already removed was quite wet
or moistened. It made the hole and removed the dirt
with its hind legs only, not using its tail or shell,
which of course could not enter the hole, though
there was some dirt on it. It first scratched two or
three times with one hind foot; then took up a pinch

of the loose sand and deposited it directly behind that leg, pushing it backward to its full length and then deliberately opening it and letting the dirt fall; then the same with the other hind foot. This it did rapidly, using each leg alternately with perfect regularity, standing on the other one the while, and thus tilting up its shell each time, now to this side, then to that. There was half a minute or a minute between each change. The hole was made as deep as the feet could reach, or about two inches. It was very neat about its work, not scattering the dirt about any more than was necessary. The completing of the hole occupied perhaps five minutes.

It then without any pause drew its head completely into its shell, raised the rear a little, and protruded and dropped a wet fleshcolored egg into the hole, one end foremost, the red skin of its body being considerably protruded with it. Then it put out its head again a little, slowly, and placed the egg at one side with one hind foot. After a delay of about two minutes it again drew in its head and dropped another, and so on to the fifth—drawing in its head each time, and pausing somewhat longer between the last. The eggs were placed in the hole without any *particular* care,—only well down flat and [each] out of the way of the next,—and I could plainly see them from above.

After these ten minutes or more, it without pause or turning began to scrape the moist earth into the hole with its hind legs, and, when it had half filled it, it carefully pressed it down with the edges of its hind feed, dancing on them alternately, for some time, as on its knees, tilting from side to side, pressing by the whole weight of the rear of its shell.

When it had drawn in thus all the earth that had
been moistened, it stretched its hind legs further
back and to each side, and drew in the dry and
lichen-clad crust, and then danced upon and pressed that down, still not moving the rear of its shell

more than one inch to right or left all the while, or
changing the position of the forward part at all. The
thoroughness with which the covering was done
was remarkable. It persevered in drawing in and
dancing on the dry surface which had never been
disturbed, long after you thought it had done its du-
ty, but it never moved its fore feet, nor once looked round, nor saw the eggs it had laid. There were
frequent pauses throughout the whole, when it
rested, or ran out its head and looked about cir-
cumspectly, at any noise or motion. These pauses
were especially long during the covering of the eggs,
which occupied more than half an hour. Perhaps
it was hard work.

When it had done, it immediately started for the river at a pretty rapid rate (the suddenness with which it made these transitions was amusing), pausing from time to time, and I judged that it would reach it in fifteen minutes. It was not easy to detect that the ground had been disturbed there. An Indian could not have made his cache more skillfully. In a few minutes all traces of it would be lost to the eye. The object of moistening the earth was perhaps to enable it to take it up in its hands (?), and also to prevent its falling back into the hole. Perhaps it also helped to make the ground more compact and harder when it was pressed down.

October 28, 1855. As I paddle under the Hemlock bank this cloudy afternoon, about 3 o'clock, I see a screech owl sitting on the edge of a hollow hemlock stump about three feet high, at the base of a large hemlock. It sits with its head drawn in, eying me, with its eyes partly open, about twenty feet off. When it hears me move, it turns its head toward me, perhaps one eye only open, with its great glaring golden iris. You see two whitish triangular lines above the eyes meeting at the bill, with a sharp reddish-brown triangle between and a narrow curved line of black under each eye. At this distance and in this light, you see only a black spot where the eye is, and the question is whether the eyes are open or not. It sits on the lee side of the tree this raw and windy day. You would say that this was a bird without a neck. Its short bill, which rests upon its breast, scarcely projects at all, but in a state of rest the whole upper part of the bird from the wings is rounded off smoothly, excepting the horns, which stand up conspicuously or are slanted back. After watching it ten minutes from the boat, I landed two rods above, and, stealing quietly up behind the hemlock, though from the windward, I looked carefully around it, and, to my surprise, saw the owl sitting there. So I sprang round quickly, with my arm outstretched, and caught it in my hand. It was so surprised that it offered no resistance at first, only glared at me in mute astonishment with eyes as big as saucers. But ere long it began to snap it's bill, making quite a noise, and, as I rolled it up in my handkerchief and put it in my pocket, it bit my finger slightly. I soon took it out of my pocket and tying the handkerchief, left it on the bottom of the boat. So I carried it home and made a small cage in which to keep it, for a night. When I took it up it clung so tightly to my hand as to sink its claws into my fingers and bring blood.

When alarmed or provoked most, it snaps its bill and hisses. It puffs up its feathers to nearly twice

its usual size, stretches out its neck, and, with wide-open eyes, stares this way and that, moving its head slowly and undulatingly from side to side with a curious motion. While I write this evening, I see that there is ground for much superstition in it. It looks out on me from a dusky corner of its box with its great solemn eyes, so perfectly still itself. I was surprised to find that I could imitate its noise as I remember it, by a *gutteral* whinnering.

A remarkably squat figure, being very broad in proportion to its length, with a short tail, and very catlike in the face with its horns and great eyes. Remarkably large feet and talons, legs thickly clothed and whitish down, down to the talons. It brought blood from my fingers by clinging to them. It would lower its head, stretch out its neck, and, bending it from side to side, peer at you with laughable circumspection; from side to side, as if to catch or absorb into its eyes every ray of light, strain at you with complacent yet earnest scrutiny. Raising and lowering its head and moving it from side to side in a slow and regular manner, at the same time snapping its bill smartly perhaps, and faintly hissing, and puffing itself up more and more,—cat-like, turtle-like, both in hissing and swelling. The slowness and gravity, not to say solemnity, of this motion are striking. There plainly is no jesting in this case. . .

General color of the owl a rather pale and perhaps slightly reddish brown, the feathers centred with black. Perches with two claws above and two below the perch. It is a slight body, covered with a mass of soft and light-lying feathers. Its head muffled in a great hood. It must be quite comfortable in winter. Dropped a pellet of fur and bones (?) in his cage. He sat, not really moping but trying to sleep, in a corner of his box all day, yet with one or both eyes slightly open all the while. I never once caught him with his eyes shut. Ordinarily stood rather than sat on his perch.

*O**ctober 29, 1855.* P.M. Up Assabet. Carried my owl to the hill again. Had to shake him out of the box, for he did not go of his own accord. (He had learned to alight on his perch, and it was surprising how lightly and noiselessly he would hop upon it.) There he stood on the grass, at first bewildered, with his horns pricked up and looking toward me. In this strong light the pupils of his eyes suddenly contracted and the iris expanded till they were two great brazen orbs with a centre spot merely. His attitude expressed astonishment more than anything. I was obliged to toss him up a little that he might feel his wings, and then he flapped away low and heavily to a hickory on the hillside twenty rods off. (I had let him out in the plain just east of the hill.) Thither I followed and tried to start him again. He was now on the *qui vive*, yet would not start. He erected his head, showing some neck, narrower than the round head above. His eyes were broad brazen rings around bullets of black. His horns stood quite an inch high, as not

before. As I moved around him, he turned his head always toward me, till he looked *directly* behind himself as he sat crosswise on a bough. He behaved as if bewildered and dazzled, gathering all the light he could and ever straining his great eyes toward [you] to make out who you are, but not inclining to fly. I had to lift him again with a stick to make him fly, and then he only rose to a higher perch, where at last he seemed to seek a shelter of a thicker cluster of the sere leaves, partly crouching there. He never appeared so much alarmed as surprised and astonished.

When I first saw him yesterday, he sat on the edge of a hollow hemlock stump about three feet high, at the bottom of a large hemlock, amid the darkness of the evergreens that cloudy day. (It threatened to rain every moment.) At the bottom of the hollow, or eighteen inches beneath him, was a very soft bed of the fine green moss (hypnum) which grows on the bank close by, probably his own bed. It had been recently put there.

When I moved him in his cage he would cling to the perch, though it was in a perpendicular position, one foot above another, suggesting his habit of clinging to and climbing the inside of hollow trees. I do not remember any perpendicular line in his eyes, as in those of the cat.

*N*ovember 9, 1855. Saw in the pool at the Hemlocks what I at first thought was a brighter leaf moved by the zephyr on the surface of the smooth dark water, but it was a splendid male summer duck, [wood duck] which allowed us to approach within seven or eight rods, sailing up close to the shore, and then rose and flew up the curving stream. We soon overhauled it again, and got a fair and long view of it. It was a splendid bird, a perfect floating gem, and [H.G.O.] Blake, who had never seen the like, was greatly surprised, not knowing that so splendid a bird was found in this part of the world. There it was, constantly moving back and forth by invisible means and wheeling on the smooth surface, showing now its breast, now its side, now its rear. It had a large, rich, flowing, green burnished crest,—a most ample headdress,—two crescents of dazzling white on the side of the head and the black neck, a pinkish (?)-red bill (with black tip) and similar irises, and a long white mark under and at wing point on sides; the side, as if the form of wing at this distance, light bronze or greenish brown; but, above all, its breast, when it turns into the right light, all aglow with splendid purple (?) or ruby (?) reflections, *like the throat of the humming-bird*. It might not appear so close at hand. This was the most surprising to me. What an ornament to a river to see that glowing gem floating in contact with its waters! As if the hummingbird should recline its ruby throat and its breast on the water. Like dipping a glowing coal in water! It so affected me.

It became excited, fluttered or flapped its wings with a slight whistling noise, and arose and flew two or three rods and alighted. It sailed close up to the edge of a rock, by which it lay pretty still, and finally sailed fast up one side of the river by the willows, etc., off the duck swamp beyond the spring, now and then turning and sailing back a foot or two, while we paddled up the opposite side a rod in the

rear, for twenty or thirty rods. At length we went by it, and it flew back low a few rods to where we roused it. It never offered to dive. We came equally near it again on our return. Unless you are thus near, and have a glass, the splendor and beauty of its colors will not be discovered. . .

That duck was all jewels combined, showing different lustres as it turned on the unrippled element in various lights, now brilliant glossy green, now dusky violet, now a rich bronze, now the reflections that sleep in the ruby's grain.

February 11, 1856. Saw a partridge by the riverside, opposite Fair Haven Hill, which at first I mistook for the top of a fencepost above the snow, amid some alders. I shouted and waved my hand four rods off, to see if it was one, but there was no motion, and I thought surely it must be a post. Nevertheless I resolved to investigate. Within three rods, I saw it to be indeed a partridge, to my surprise, standing perfectly still, with its head erect and neck stretched upward. It was as complete a deception as if it had designedly placed itself on the line of the fence and in the proper place for a post. It finally stepped off daintily with a teetering gait and head up, and took to wing.

*M**arch 23, 1856.* As I was returning on the railroad, at the crossing beyond the shanty, hearing a rustling, I saw a striped squirrel amid the sedge on the bare east bank, twenty feet distant. After observing me a few moments, as I stood perfectly still between the rails, he ran straight up to within three feet of me, out of curiosity; then, after a moment's pause, and looking up to my face, turned back and finally crossed the railroad. All the red was on his rump and hind quarters. When running he carried his tail erect, as he scratched up the snowy bank.

*M**ay 18, 1856. Sailed* back on Hubbard's redstart path, and there saw a mud turtle draw in his head, of which I saw the half, about eight rods off. Pushed to the spot, where the water was about a foot deep, and at length detected him spread out on the bottom, his monstrous head and tail and legs outspread, probably directly under where he had appeared. At first, I suspect, I mistook him for a rock, for he was thickly covered with a short green moss-like conferva (?),—a venerable object, a true son of the meadow, suggesting what vigor! what naturalness! Perchance to make the moss grow on your back without injuring your health! How many things can he sustain on his shell where the mosses grow? He looked like an antediluvian under that green, shaggy shell, tougher than the rock you mistake it for. No wonder the Indian reverenced him as a god. Think of the time when he was an infant. There is your native American, who was before Columbus, perchance. Grown, not gray, but green with the lapse of ages. Living with the life of the meadow. I took off my coat, stripped up my shirt-sleeve, and caught him by his great rough tail. He snapped at me and my paddle, striking his snout against the side of the boat till he made it bleed. Though I held him down with an oar for a lever and my foot on it, he would suddenly lift all together, or run out his head and knock the oar and my leg aside. He held up his head to me and, with his mouth wide open, hissed in his breathing like a locomotive for a quarter of an hour, and I could look straight down his monstrous gullet ten inches. The only way to hold him and paddle too was to turn him on his back, then, putting the end of a paddle under a seat, slant it over his sternum and press my foot on the other end. He was fourteen and one half inches long by twelve at the broadest places, and weighed twenty-five pounds and three ounces. The claws were an inch and a quarter long beyond the skin, and very stout. You had to exert yourself to turn him over on a plane surface, he held down so firmly with his claws, as if grown to it. He took my hand into his shell with his tail and took the skin off it. The sternum is broadest forward. This turtle was not roundish like the shell I have, but nearly an oblong square; nearly as long as that, but much less wide. The usual number of scallops behind.

I know of a young lady who, when riding, came across one in the road, which not wishing to run over, she got out and tried to drive it out of the way with her whip, but it "screamed" at and terrified her. A caravan could not make him budge under those circumstances.

May, 20, 1856. After I got him home, I observed a large leech on the upper shell of my great turtle. He stoutly resisted being turned over, by sinking his claws into the ground; was aware that that was his weak side, and, when turned, would instantly run out his head and turn himself back. No wonder the Orientals rested the world on such a broad back. Such broad health and strength underlies Nature.

June 6, 1856. In the large circular hole or cellar at the turntable on the railroad, which they are repairing, I see a starnosed mole endeavoring in vain to bury himself in the sandy and gravelly bottom. Some inhuman fellow has cut off his tail. It is blue-black with much fur, a very thick, plump animal, apparently some four inches long, but he occasionally shortens himself a third or more. Looks as fat as a fat hog. His fore feet are large and set sidewise or on their edges, and with these he shovels the earth aside, while his large, long, starred snout is feeling the way and breaking ground. I see deep indentations in his fur where his eyes are situated, and once I saw distinctly his eye open, a dull blue (?)-black bead, not so very small, and he very plainly noticed my movements two feet off. He was using his eye as plainly as any creature that I ever saw. Yet [Ebenezer] Emmons says it is a question whether their eyes are not merely rudimentary. I suppose this was the *Condylura macroura*, since that is the most common, but only an inch of its tail was left, and that was quite stout. I carried him along to plowed ground, where he buried himself in a minute or two.

June 10, 1856. A painted tortoise laying her eggs ten feet from the wheel-track on the Marlborough road. She paused at first, but I sat down within two feet, and she soon resumed her work. Had excavated a hollow about five inches wide and six long in the moistened sand, and cautiously, with long intervals, she continued her work, resting always on the same spot her fore feet, and never looking round, her eye shut all but a narrow slit. Whenever I moved, perhaps to brush off a mosquito, she paused. A wagon approached, rumbling afar off, and then there was a pause, till it had passed and long, long after, a tedious, *naturlangsam* pause of the slow-blooded creature, a sacrifice of time such as those animals are up to which slumber half a year and live for centuries. It was twenty minutes before I discovered that she was not making the hole but filling it up slowly, having laid her eggs. She drew the moistened sand under herself, scraping it along from behind with both feet brought together, the claws turned inward. In the long pauses the ants troubled her (as mosquitoes me) by running over her eyes, which made her snap or dart out her head suddenly, striking the shell. She did not dance on the sand, nor finish covering the hollow quite so carefully as the one observed last year. She went off suddenly (and quickly at first), with a slow but sure instinct through the wood toward the swamp.

July 19, 1856. 5 P.M. Up Assabet. As I was bathing under the swamp white oaks at 6 P.M., heard a suppressed sound often repeated, like, perhaps, the working of beer through a bung-hole, which I already suspected to [be] produced by owls. I was uncertain whether it was far or near. Proceeding a dozen rods up-stream on the south side, toward where a catbird was incessantly mewing, I found myself suddenly within a rod of a gray screech owl sitting on an alder bough with horns erect, turning its head from side to side and up and down, and peering at me in that same ludicrously solemn and complacent way that I had noticed in one in captivity. Another, more red, also horned, repeated the same warning sound, or apparently call to its young, about the same distance off, in another direction, on an alder. When they took to flight they made some noise with their wings. With their short tails and squat figures they looked very clumsy, all head and shoulders. Hearing a fluttering under the alders, I drew near and found a young owl, a third smaller than the old, all gray, without obvious horns, only four or five feet distant. It flitted along two rods, and I followed it. I saw at least two or more young. All this was close by that thick hemlock grove, and they perched on alders and an apple tree in the thicket there. These birds kept opening their eyes when I moved, as if to get clearer sight of me. The young were very quick to notice any motion of the old, and so betrayed their return by looking in that direction when they returned, though I had not heard it. Though they permitted me to come so near with so much noise, as if bereft of half their senses, they at [once] noticed the coming and going of the old birds, even when I did not. There were four or five owls in all. I have heard a somewhat similar note, further off and louder, in the night.

July 15, 1856. When I crossed the entrance to the pond meadow on a stick, a pout ran ashore and was lodged so that I caught it in the grass, apparently frightened. While I held it, I noticed another, a very large one approach the shore very boldly within a few feet of me. Going in to bathe, I caught a pout on the bottom within a couple of rods of the shore. It seemed sick. Then, wading into the shallow entrance of the meadow, I saw a school of a thousand little pouts about three quarters of an inch long without any attending pout, and now have no doubt that the pout I had caught (but let go again) was tending them, and the large one was the father, apparently further off. The mother had perhaps gone into deep water to recruit after her air-bath. The young were pretty shy; kept in shallow water, and were taking pretty good care of themselves. If the water should suddenly fall, they might be caught in the meadow.

June 24, 1857. Went to Farmer's Swamp to look for the screech owl's [The situation of the nest and Thoreau's description of the notes indicate a long-eared owl rather than a screech owl.] nest Farmer had found. You go about forty-five rods on the first path to the left in the woods and then turn to the left a few rods. I found the nest at last near the top of a middling-sized white pine, about thirty feet from the ground. As I stood by the tree, the old bird dashed by within a couple of rods, uttering a peculiar mewing sound, which she kept up amid the bushes, a blackbird in close pursuit of her. I found the nest empty, on one side of the main stem but close to it, resting on some limbs. It was made of twigs rather less than an eighth of an inch thick and was almost flat above, only an inch lower in the middle than at the edge, about sixteen inches in diameter and six or eight inches thick, with the twigs in the midst, and beneath was mixed sphagnum and sedge from the swamp beneath, and the lining or flooring was coarse strips of grape-vine bark; the whole pretty firmly matted together. How common and important a material is grape-vine bark for birds' nests! Nature wastes nothing. There were white droppings of the young on the nest and one large pellet of fur and small bones two and a half inches long. In the meanwhile, the old bird was uttering that hoarse worried note from time to time, somewhat like a partridge's, flying past from side to side and alighting amid the trees or bushes. When I had descended, I detected one young, one two thirds grown perched on a branch of the next tree, about fifteen feet from the ground, which was all the while staring at me with its great yellow eyes. It was gray with gray horns and a dark beak. As I walked past near it, it turned its head steadily, always facing me, without moving its body, till it looked directly the opposite way over its back, but never offered to fly. Just then I thought surely that I heard a puppy faintly barking at me four or five rods distant amid the bushes, having tracked me into the swamp,—*what what, what what what.* It was exactly such a noise as the barking of a very small dog or perhaps a fox. But it was the old owl, for I

presently saw her making it. She repeated [*sic*] perched quite near. She was generally reddish-brown or partridge-colored, the breast mottled with dark brown and fawn-color in the downward strings [*sic*], and had plain fawn-colored thighs.

September 12, 1857. Saturday. P.M. To Owl Swamp (Farmer's). In an open part of the swamp, started a very large wood frog, which gave one leap and squatted still. I put down my finger, and, though it shrank a little at first, it permitted me to stroke it as long as I pleased. Having passed, it occurred to me to return and cultivate its acquaintance. To my surprise, it allowed me to slide my hand under it and lift it up, while it squatted cold and moist on the middle of my palm, panting naturally. I brought it close to my eye and examined it. It was very beautiful seen thus nearly, not the dull dead-leaf color which I had imagined, but its back was like burnished bronze armor defined by a varied line on each side, where, as it seemed, the plates of armor united. It had four or five dusky bars which matched exactly when the legs were folded, showing that the painter applied his brush to the animal when in that position, and reddish-orange soles to its delicate feet. There was a conspicuous dark-brown patch along the side of the head, whose upper edge passed directly through the eye horizontally, just above its centre, so that the pupil and all below were dark and the upper portion of the iris golden. I have since taken up another in the same way.

October 5, 1857. I hear the alarum of a small red squirrel. I see him running by fits and starts along a chestnut bough toward me. His head looks disproportionately large for his body, like a bulldog's, perhaps because he has his chaps full of nuts. He chirrups and vibrates his tail, holds himself in, and scratches along a foot as if it were a mile. He finds noise and activity for both of us. It is evident that all this ado does not proceed from fear. There is at the bottom, no doubt, an excess of inquisitiveness and caution, but the greater part is make-believe and a love of the marvellous. He can hardly keep it up till I am gone, however, but takes out his nut and tastes it in the midst of his agitation. *"See there, see there,"* says he, "who's that? O dear, what shall I do?" and makes believe run off, but doesn't get along an inch,—lets it all pass off by flashes through his tail, while he clings to the bark as if he were holding in a race-horse. He gets down the trunk at last on to a projecting knot, head downward, within a rod of you, and chirrups and chatters louder than ever. Tries to work himself into a fright. The hind part of his body is urging the forward part along, snapping the tail over it like a whip-lash, but the fore part, for the most part, clings fast to the bark with desperate energy. *Squirr*, "to throw with a jerk," seems to have quite as much to do with the same as the Greek *skia oura*, shadow and tail.

November 15, 1857. Going by my owl-nest oak, I saw that it had broken off at the hole and the top fallen, but, seeing in the cavity some leaves, I climbed up to see what kind of nest it was and what traces of the owls were left. Having shinnied up with some difficulty to the top of this great stump some fifteen or eighteen feet high, I took out the leaves slowly, watching to see what spoils had been left with them. Some were pretty green, and all had evidently been placed there this fall. When I had taken all out with my left hand, holding on to the top of the stump with my right, I looked round into the cleft, and there I saw, sitting nearly erect at the bottom in one corner, a little *Mus leucopus* [deer mouse], panting with fear and with its large black eyes upon me. I held my face thus within seven or eight inches of it as long as I cared to hold on there, and it showed no sign of retreating. When I put in my hand, it merely withdrew downward into a snug little nest of hypnum and apparently the dirty-white wool-like pappus of some plant as big as a battingball. Wishing to see its tail, I stirred it up again, when it suddenly rushed up the side of the cleft, out over my shoulder and right arm, and leaped off, falling down through a thin hemlock spray some fifteen or eighteen feet to the ground, on the hillside, where I lost sight of it, but heard it strike. It will thus make its nest at least sixteen feet up a tree, improving some cleft or hollow, or probably bird's nest, for this purpose. These nests, *I suppose*, are made when the trees are losing their leaves, as those of the squirrels are.

*A**pril 2, 1858.** At the spring on the west side of Fair Haven Hill, I startle a striped snake. It is a large one with a white stripe down the dorsal ridge between two broad black ones, and on each side the last a buff one, and then blotchy brown sides, darker toward tail; beneath, greenish-yellow. This snake generally has a pinkish cast. There is another, evidently the same species but not half so large, with its neck lying affectionately across the first,—I may have separated them by my approach,—which, seen by itself, you might have thought a distinct species. The dorsal line in this one is bright-yellow, though not so bright as the lateral ones, and the yellow about the head; also the black is more glossy, and this snake has no pink cast. No doubt on almost every such warm bank now you will find a snake lying out. The first notice I had of them was a slight rustling in the leaves, as if made

by a squirrel, though I did not see them for five minutes after. The biggest at length dropped straight down into a hole, within a foot of where he lay. They allowed me to lift their heads with a stick four or five inches without stirring, nor did they mind the flies that alighted on them, looking steadily at me without the slightest motion of head, body, or eyes, as if they were of marble; and as you looked hard at them, you continually forgot that they were real and not imaginary.

April 12, 1858. Returning on the railroad, the noon train down passed us opposite the old maid Hosmer's house. In the woods just this side, we came upon a partridge standing on the track, between the rails over which the cars had just passed. She had evidently been run down, but, though a few small feathers were scattered along for a dozen rods beyond her, and she looked a little ruffled, she was apparently more disturbed in mind than body. I took her up and carried her one side to a safer place. At first she made no resistance, but at length fluttered out of my hands and ran two or three feet.

I had to take her up again and carry and drive her further off, and left her standing with head erect as at first, as if beside herself. She was not lame, and I suspect no wing was broken. I did not suspect that this swift wild bird was ever run down by the cars. We have an account in the newspapers of every cow and calf that is run over, but not of the various wild creatures who meet with that accident. It may be many generations before the partridges learn to give the cars a sufficiently wide berth.

A *pril 15, 1858.* Having stood quite still on the edge of the ditch close to the north edge of the maple swamp some time, and heard a slight rustling near me from time to time, I looked round and saw a mink under the bushes within a few feet. It was pure reddish-brown above, and a blackish and somewhat bushy tail, a blunt nose, and somewhat innocent-looking head. It crept along toward me and around me, *within two feet*, in a semi-circle, snuffing the air, and pausing to look at me several times. Part of its course when nearest me was in the water of the ditch. It then crawled slowly away, and

I saw by the ripple where it had taken to the ditch again. Perhaps it was after a frog, like myself. It may have been attracted by the peeping. But how much blacker was the creature I saw April 28th, 1857! A very different color, though the tail the same form.

The naturalist accomplishes a great deal by patience, more perhaps than by activity. He must take his position, and then wait and watch. It is equally true of quadrupeds and reptiles. Sit still in the midst of their haunts.

*A**pril 18, 1858.*** Frogs are strange creatures. One would describe them as particularly wary and timid, another as equally bold and imperturbable. All that is required in studying them is patience. You will sometimes walk a long way along a ditch and hear twenty or more leap in one after another before you, and see where they rippled the water, without getting sight of one of them. Sometimes, as this afternoon the two *R. fontinalis*, when you approach a pool or spring a frog hops in and buries itself at the bottom. You sit down on the brink and wait patiently for his reappearance. After a quarter of an hour or more he is sure to rise to the surface and put out his nose quietly without making a ripple, eying you steadily. At length he becomes as curious about you as you can be about him. He suddenly hops straight toward [you], pausing within a foot, and takes a near and leisurely view of you. Perchance you may now scratch its nose with your finger and examine it to your heart's content, for it is become as imperturbable as it was shy before. You conquer them by superior patience and immovableness; not by quickness, but by slowness; not by heat, but by coldness. You see only a pair of heels disappearing in the weedy bottom, and, saving a few insects, the pool becomes as smooth as a mirror and apparently as uninhabited. At length, after half an hour, you detect a frog's snout and a pair of eyes above the green slime, turned toward you,—etc.

May 13, 1858. As I sat in my boat near the Bath Rock at Island, I saw a red squirrel steal slyly up a red maple, as if he were in search of a bird's nest (though it is early for most), and I thought I would see what he was at. He crept far out on the slender branches and, reaching out his neck, nibbled off the fruit-stems, sometimes bending them within reach with his paw; and then, squatting on the twig, he voraciously devoured the half-grown keys, using his paws to direct them to his mouth, as a nut. Bunch after bunch he plucked and ate, letting many fall, and he made an abundant if not sumptuous feast, the whole tree hanging red with fruit around him. It seemed like a fairy fruit as I saw looking toward the sun and saw the red keys made all glowing and transparent by the sun between me and the body of the squirrel. It was certainly a cheering sight,a cunning red squirrel perched on a slender twig between you and the sun, feasting on the handsome red maple keys. He nibbled voraciously, as if they were a sweet and lucious fruit to him. What an abundance and variety of food is now ready for him! At length, when the wind suddenly began to blow hard and shake the twig on which he sat, he quickly ran down a dozen feet.

May 16, 1858. Sat down in the sun in the path through Wright's wood-lot above Goose Pond, but soon, hearing a slight rustling, I looked round and saw a very large black snake about five feet long on the dry leaves, about a rod off. When I moved, it vibrated its tail very rapidly and smart-

ly, which made quite a loud rustling or rattling sound, reminding me of the rattlesnake, as if many snakes obeyed the same instinct as the rattlesnake when they vibrate their tails. Once I thought I heard a low hiss. It was on the edge of a young wood of oaks and a few white pines from ten to eighteen feet high, the oaks as yet bare of leaves. As I moved toward the snake, I thought it would take refuge in some hole, but it appeared that it was out on a scout and did not know of any place of refuge near. Suddenly, as it moved along, it erected itself half its length, and when I thought it was preparing to strike at me, to my surprise it glided up a slender oak sapling about an inch in diameter at the ground and ten feet high. It ascended this easily and quickly, at first, I think, slanting its body over the lowest twig of the next tree. There were seven little branches for nine feet, averaging about the size of a pipe-stem. It moved up in a somewhat zig-zag manner, availing itself of the branches, yet also in part spirally about the main stem. It finds a rest (or hold if necessary) for its neck or forward part of its body, moving crosswise the small twigs, then draws up the rest of its body. From the top of this little oak it passed into the top of a white pine of the same height an inch and a half in diameter at the ground and two feet off; from this into another oak, fifteen feet high and three feet from the pine; from this to another oak, three feet from the last and about the same height; from this to a large oak about four feet off and three or four inches in diameter, in which it was about fourteen feet from the ground; thence through two more oaks, a little lower, at intervals of four feet, and so into a white pine; and at last into a smaller white pine and thence to the ground. The distance in a straight line from where it left the ground to where it descended was about twenty-five feet, and the greatest height it reached, about fourteen feet. It moved quite deliberately for the most part, choosing its course from tree to tree with great skill, and resting from time to time while it watched me, only my approach compelling it to move again. It surprised me very much to see it cross from tree to tree exactly like a squirrel, where there appeared little or no support for such a body. It would glide down the proper twig, its body resting at intervals of a foot or two, on the smaller side twigs, perchance, and then would easily cross an interval of two feet, sometimes in an ascending, sometimes a descending, direction. If the latter, its weight at last bent the first twig down nearer to the opposite one. It would extend its neck very much, as I could see by the increased width of the scales exposed, till its neck rested across the opposite twig, hold on all the while tightly to some part of the last twig by the very tip of its tail, which was curled round it just like a monkey's. I have hardly seen a squirrel *rest* on such slight twigs as it would rest on in midair, only two or three not bigger than a pipe stem, while its body stretched *clear* a foot at least between two trees. It was not at all like creeping over a coarse basketwork, but suggested long practice and skill, like the rope-dancer's. There were no limbs for it to use comparable for size with its own body, and you hardly noticed the few slight twigs it rested on, as it glided through the air. When its neck rested on the opposite twig, it was, as it were glued to it. It helped itself over or up them as surely as if it grasped with a hand. There were, no doubt, rigid kinks in its body when they were needed for support. It is a sort of endless hook, and, by its ability to bend its body in every direction, it finds some support on every side. Perhaps the edges of its scales give it a hold also. It is evident that it can take the young birds out of a sapling of any height, and no twigs are so small and pliant as to prevent it. Pendulous sprays would be the most difficult for it, where the twigs are more nearly parallel with the main one, as well as nearly vertical, but even then it might hold on by its tail while its head hung below. I have no doubt that this snake could have reached many of the oriole-nests which I have seen. I noticed that in its anger its rigid neck was very much flattened or compressed vertically. At length it coiled upon itself as if to strike, and, I presenting a stick, it struck it smartly and then darted away, running swiftly down the hill toward the pond.

May 20, 1858. Going along the deep valley in the woods, just before entering the part called Laurel Glen, I heard a noise, and saw a fox running off along the shrubby side-hill. It looked like a rather small dirty-brown fox, and very clumsy, running much like a woodchuck. It had a dirty or dark brown tail, with very little white to the tip. A few steps further I came upon the remains of a woodchuck, yet warm, which it had been eating. Head, legs, and tail, all remained, united by the skin, but the bowels and a good part of the flesh were eaten. This was evidently a young fox, say three quarters grown, or perhaps less, and appeared as full as a tick. There was a fox-hole within three rods, with a very large sand-heap, several cartloads, before it, much trodden. Hearing a bird of which I was in search, I turned to examine it, when I heard a bark behind me, and, looking round, saw an old fox on the brow of the hill on the west side of the valley, amid the bushes, about ten rods off, looking down at me. At first it was a short, puppy-like bark, but afterward it began to bark on a higher key and more prolonged, very unlike a dog, a very ragged half-screaming *bur-ar-r-r*. I proceeded along the valley half a dozen rods after a little delay (the fox being gone), and then looked round to see if it returned to the woodchuck. I then saw a full-grown fox, perhaps the same as the last, cross the valley through the thin low wood fifteen or twenty rods behind me, but from east to west, pausing and looking at me anxiously from time to time. It was rather light tawny (not fox-colored) with dusky-brown bars, and looked very large, wolf-like. The full-grown fox stood much higher on its legs and was longer, but the body was apparently not much heavier than that of the young. Going a little further, I came to another hole, and ten feet off was a space of a dozen square feet amid some little oaks, worn quite bare and smooth, apparently by the playing of the foxes, and the ground close around a large stump about a rod from the hole was worn bare and hard, and all the bark and much of the rotten wood was pawed or gnawed off lately. They had pawed a deep channel about one and in between the roots, perhaps for insects. There lay the remains of another woodchuck, now dry, the head, skin, and legs being left, and also part of the skin of a third, and the bones of another animal, and some partridge feathers. The old foxes had kept their larder well supplied. Within a rod was another hole, apparently a back door, having no heap of sand, and five or six rods off another in the side of the hill with a small sand-heap and a back door with none. There was a well-beaten path from the one on the side-hill five or six rods long to one in the valley, and there was much blackish dung about the holes and stump and the path. By the hole furthest down the valley was another stump, which had been gnawed (?) very much and trampled and pawed about like the other. I suppose the young foxes play there. There were half a dozen holes or more, and what with the skulls and feathers and skin and bones about, I was reminded of Golgotha. These holes were some of them very large and conspicuous, a foot wide vertically, by eight or ten inches, going into the side-hill with a curving stoop, and there was commonly a very large heap of sand before them, trodden smooth. It was a sprout-land valley, cut off but a year or two since. As I stood by the last hole, I heard the old fox bark, and saw her (?) near the brow of the hill on the north-west, amid the bushes, restless and anxious, overlooking me a dozen or fourteen rods off. I was, no doubt, by the hole in which the young were. She uttered at very short intervals a prolonged, shrill, screeching kind of bark, beginning lower and rising to a very high key, lasting two seconds; a very broken and ragged sound, more like the scream of a large and angry bird than the bark of a dog, trilled like a piece of vibrating metal at the end. It moved restlessly back and forth, or approached nearer, and stood or sat on its haunches like a dog with its tail laid out in a curve on one side, and when it barked it laid its ears flat back and stretched its nose forward. Sometimes it uttered a short, puppy-like, snappish bark. It was not fox-colored now, but a very light tawny or wolf-color, dark-brown or dusky beneath in a broad line from its throat; its legs the same, with a broad dusky perpendicular band on its haunches and similar ones on

its tail, and a small whitish spot on each side of its mouth. There it sat like a chieftain on his hills, looking, methought, as big as a prairie wolf, and shaggy like it, anxious and even fierce, as I peered through my glass. I noticed, when it withdrew,—I too withdrawing in the opposite direction,—that as it had descended the hill a little way and wanted to go off over the pinnacle without my seeing which way it went, it ran one side about ten feet, till it was behind a small white pine, then turned at a right angle and ascended the hill directly, with the pine between us. The sight of it suggested that two or three might attack a man. The note was a shrill, vibrating scream or cry; could easily be heard a quarter of a mile. How many woodchucks, rabbits, partridges, etc., etc., they must kill, and yet how few of them are seen! A very wolfish color. It must have been a large fox, and, if it is true that the old are white on the sides of the face, an old one. They evidently used more than a half dozen holes within fifteen rods. I withdrew the sooner for fear by his barking he would be betrayed to some dog or gunner.

It was a very wild sight to see the wolf-like parent circling about me in the thin wood, from time to time pausing to look and bark at me. This appears to be nearest to the cross fox of Audubon, and is considered a variety of the red by him and most others, not white beneath as the red fox of [Richard] Harlan. Emmons says of the red fox, "In the spring the color appears to fade," and that some are "pale yellow," but does not describe minutely. This was probably a female, for [Thomas] Bell says of the English fox that the female "loses all her timidity and shyness when suckling her young;" also that they are a year and a half in attaining their full size.

June 7, 1858. As I was wading in this Wyman meadow, looking for bullfrog-spawn, I saw a hole at the bottom, where it was six or eight inches deep, by the side of a mass of mud and weeds which rose just to the surface three or four feet from the shore. It was about five inches in diameter, with some sand at the mouth, just like a musquash's hole. As I stood there within two feet, a pout put her head out, as if to see who was there, and directly came forth and disappeared under the target-weed; but as I stood perfectly still, waiting for the water which I had disturbed to settle about the hole, she circled round and round several times between me and the hole, cautiously, stealthily approaching the entrance but as often withdrawing, and at last mustered courage to enter it. I then noticed another similar hole in the same mass, two or three feet from this. I thrust my arm into the first, running it in and downward about fifteen inches. It was a little more than a foot long and enlarged somewhat at the end, the bottom, also, being about a foot beneath the surface,—for it slanted downward,—I felt nothing within; I only felt a pretty regular and rounded apartment with firm walls of weedy or fibrous mud. I then thrust my arm into the other hole, which was

longer and deeper, but at first discovered nothing; but, trying again, I found that I had not reached the end, for it turned a little and descended more than I supposed. Here I felt a similar apartment or enlargement, some six inches in diameter horizontally but not quite so high or nearly so wide at its throat. Here, to my surprise, I felt something soft, like a gelatinous mass of spawn, but, feeling a little further, felt the horns of a pout. I deliberately took hold of her by the head and lifted her out of the hole and in the water, having run my arm in two thirds its length. She offered not the slightest resistance from first to last, even when I held her out of water before my face, and only darted away suddenly when I dropped her in the water. The entrance to her apartment was so narrow that she could hardly have escaped if I had tried to prevent her. Putting in my arm again, I felt, under where she had been, a flattish mass of ova, several inches in diameter, resting on the mud, and took out some. Feeling again in the first hole, I found as much more there. Though I had been stepping round and over the second nest for several minutes, I had not scared the pout. The ova of the first nest already contained white wiggling young. I saw no motion in the others. The ova in each case were dullyellowish and the size of small buckshot. These nests did not communicate with each other and had no other outlet.

Pouts, then, make their nests in shallow mudholes or bays, in masses of weedy mud, or probably in the muddy bank; and the old pout hovers over the spawn or keeps guard at the entrance. Where do the Walden pouts breed when they have not access to this meadow? The first pout, whose eggs were most developed, was the largest and had some slight wounds on the back. The other may have been the male in the act of fertilizing the ova.

July 21, 1858. Wednesday. Concord, P.M.— To Walden, with E.[dward] Bartlett and E.[dward] Emerson. The former wished to show me what he thought an owl's nest he had found. Near it, in Abel Brooks's woodlot, heard a note and saw a small hawk fly over. It was the nest of this bird. Saw several of the young flitting about and occasionally an old bird. The nest was in a middling-sized white pine, some twenty feet from the ground, resting on two limbs close to the main stem, on the south side of it. It was quite solid, composed entirely of twigs about as big round as a pipe-stem and less; was some fifteen inches in diameter and one inch deep, or nearly flat, and perhaps five inches thick. It was very much dirtied on the sides by the droppings of the young. As we were standing about

the tree, we heard again the note of a young one approaching. We dropped upon the ground, and it alighted on the edge of the nest; another alighted near by, and a third a little further off. The young were apparently as big as the old, but still lingered about the nest and returned to it. I could hear them coming some distance off. Their note was a kind of peeping squeal, which you might at first suspect to be made by a jay; not very loud, but as if to attract the old and reveal their whereabouts. The note of the old bird, which occasionally dashed past, was somewhat like that of the marsh hawk or pigeon woodpecker, a cackling or clattering sound, chiding us. The old bird was anxious about her inexperienced young, and was trying to get them off. At length she dashed close past us, and appeared to fairly strike one of the young, knocking him off his perch, and he soon followed her off. I saw the remains of several birds lying about in that neighborhood, and saw and heard again the young and old thereabouts for several days thereafter. A young man killed one of the young hawks, and I saw it. It was the *Falco juscus,* the American brown or slate-colored hawk. Its length was thirteen inches; alar extent, twenty-three. The tail reached two or more inches beyond the closed wings. Nuttal says the upper parts are ''a deep slate-color'' (these were very dark brown); also that the nest is yet unknown. But Wilson describes his *F. velox* (which is the same as Nuttal's *F. juscus)* as ''whole upper parts very dark brown,'' but legs, greenish-yellow (these were yellow). The toes had the peculiar pendulous lobes which W. refers to. As I saw it in the woods, I was struck by its dark color above, its tawny throat and breast, brown-spotted, its clean, slender, long yellow legs, feathered but little below the knee, its white vent, its wings distinctly and rather finely dark-barred beneath, short, black, much curved bill, and slender black sharp claws. Its tail with a dark bar near edge beneath. In hand I found it had the white spots on scapulars of the *F. juscus,* and had not the white bars on tail of the *F. Pennsylvanicus.* It also had the fine sharp shin.

S *eptember 3, 1858.* P.M. Up Assabet a-hazelnutting. I see a small striped snake, some fifteen or eighteen inches long, swallowing a toad, all but the head and one fore leg taken in. It is a singular sight, that of the little head of the snake directly above the great, solemn, granitic head of the toad, whose eyes are open, though I have reason to think that he is not alive, for when I return some hours after I find that the snake has disgorged the toad and departed. The toad had been swallowed with the hind legs stretched out and close together, and its body is compressed and elongated to twice its length, while the head, which had not been taken in, is of the original size and full of blood. The toad is quite dead, apparently killed by being so far crushed; and its eyes are still open. The body of the snake was enlarged regularly from near the middle to its jaws. It appeared to have given up this attempt at the eleventh hour. Probably the toad is very much more elongated when perfectly swallowed by a small snake. It would seem, then, that snakes under-take to swallow toads which are too big for them.

M *arch 30, 1859.* 6 A.M. To Hill (across water). Hear a red squirrel chirrup at me by the hemlocks (running up a hemlock), all for my benefit; not that he is excited by fear, I think, but so full is he of animal spirits that he makes a great ado about the least event. At first he scratches on the bark very rapidly with his hind feet without moving the fore feet. He makes so many queer sounds, and so different from one another, that you

would think they came from half a dozen creatures. I hear now two sounds from him of a very distinct character,—a low or base inward, worming, screwing, or brewing, kind of sound (very like that, by the way, which an anxious partridge mother makes) and at the same time a very sharp and shrill bark, and clear, on a very high key, totally distinct from the last,—while his tail is flashing incessantly. You might say that he successfully accomplished the difficult feat of singing and whistling at the same time.

*A**pril 7, 1859.*** Standing under the north side of the hill, I hear the rather innocent *phe phe, phe phe, phe phe, phé,* of a fish hawk (for is it not a scream, but a rather soft and innocent note), and, looking up, see one come sailing from over the hill. The body looks quite short in proportion to the spread of the wings, which are quite dark or blackish above. He evidently has something in his talons. We soon after disturb him again, and, at length, after circling around over the hill and adjacent fields, he alights in plain sight on one of the halfdead white oaks on the top of the hill, where probably he sat before. As I look through my glass, he is perched on a large dead limb and is evidently standing on a fish (I had noticed something in his talons as he flew), for he stands high and uneasily, finding it hard to keep his balance in the wind. He is disturbed by our neighborhood and does not proceed at once to eat his meal. I see the tail of the fish hanging over the end of the limb. Now and then he pecks at it. I see the white on the crown of the hawk. It is a very large black bird as seen against the sky. Soon he sails away again, carrying his fish, as before, horizontally beneath his body, and he circles about over the adjacent pasture like a hawk hunting, though he can only be looking for a suitable place to eat his fish or waiting for us to be gone.

Looking under the limb on which he was perched, we find a piece of the skin of a sucker (?) or some other scaly fish which a hawk had dropped there long since. No doubt many a fish hawk has taken his meal on that sightly perch.

It seems, then, that the fish hawk which you see soaring and sailing so leisurely about over the land—for this one soared quite high into the sky at one time—may have a fish in his talons all the while and only be waiting till you are gone for an opportunity to eat it on his accustomed perch.

May 28, 1859. At the extreme side of Trillium Wood, come upon a black snake, which at first keeps still prudently, thinking I may not see him,—in the grass in open land,—then glides to the edge of the wood and darts swiftly up into the top of some slender shrubs there—*Viburnum dentatum* and alder—and lies stretched out, eying me, in horizontal loops eight feet high.

The biggest shrub was not over one inch thick at the ground. At first I thought its neck was its chief member,—as if it drew itself up by it,—but again I thought that it rather (when I watched it ascending) extended its neck and a great part of its body upward, while the lower extremity was more or less coiled and rigid on the twigs from a *point d'appui.* Thus it lifted itself quickly to higher forks. When it moved along more horizontally, it extended its neck far, and placed it successively between the slender forks. This snake, some four feet long, rested there at length twelve feet high, on twigs, not one so big as a pipe-stem, in the top of a shad-bush; yet this one's tail was broken off where a third of an inch thick, and it could not cling with that. It was quick as thought in its motions there, and perfectly at home in the trees, so far was it from making the impression of a snake in an awkward position.

May 30, 1859. When I entered the interior meadow of Gowing's Swamp I heard a slight snort, and found that I had suddenly come upon a woodchuck amid the sphagnum, lambkill, *Kalmia glauca*, andromeda, cranberry, etc., there. It was only seven feet off, and, being surprised, would not run. It would only stand erect from time to time,—

perfectly erect with its blackish paws held like hands
near together in front,—just so as to bring its head,
or eyes, above the level of the lambkill, kalmia, etc.,
and looking round, turning now this ear toward me,
then that; and every now and then it would make
a short rush at me, half a foot or so, with a snort,
and then draw back, and also grit its teeth—which
showed—very audibly, with a rattling sound,
evidently to intimidate me. I could not drive it, but
it would steadily face me and rush toward me thus.
Also it made a short motion occasionally as if to bury
itself by burrowing there. It impressed me as a
singularly wild and grizzly [*sic*] native, survivor of
the red man. He may have thought that no one but
he came to Gowing's Swamp these afternoons.

Its colors were gray, reddish brown, and
blackish, the graytipped wind hairs giving it a grizzly

look above, and when it stood up its distinct rust-color beneath was seen, while the top of its head was dark-brown, becoming black at [the] snout, as also its paws and its little rounded ears. Its head from snout to ears, when it stood up erect, made a nearly horizontal line. It did much looking round. When thus erect, its expression and posture were very bear-like, with the clumsiness of the bear. Though I drew off three or four rods, it would not retreat into the thicket (which was only a rod off) while I was there so near.

June 19, 1859. A flying squirrel's nest and young on Emerson's hatchet path, south of Walden, on hilltop, in a covered hollow in a small old stump at base of a young oak, covered with fallen leaves and a portion of the stump; nest apparently of dry grass. Saw three young run out after the mother and up a slender oak. The young half-grown, very tender-looking and weak-tailed, yet one climbed quite to the top of an oak twenty-five feet high, though feebly. Claws must be very sharp and early developed. The mother rested quite near, on a small projecting stub big as a pipe-stem, curled crosswise on it. Have a more rounded head and snout than our other squirrels. The young in danger of being picked off by hawks.

August 14, 1859. When I reached the upper end of this weedy bar, at about 3 P.M., this warm day, I noticed some light-colored object in mid-river, near the other end of the bar. At first I thought of some large stake or board standing amid the weeds there, then of a fisherman in a brown holland sack, referring him to the shore beyond.

Supposing it the last, I floated nearer and nearer till I saw plainly enough the motions of the person, whoever it was, and that it was no stake. Looking through my glass thirty or forty rods off, I thought certainly that I saw C., who had just bathed, making signals to me with his towel, for I referred the object to the shore twenty rods further. I saw his motions as he wiped himself,—the movements of his elbows and his towel. Then I saw that the person was nearer and therefore smaller, that it stood on the sand-bar in mid-stream in shallow water and must be some maiden [in] a bathing-dress,—for it was the color of brown holland web,—and a very peculiar kind of dress it seemed. But about this time I discovered with my naked eye that it was a blue heron standing in very shallow water amid the weeds of the bar and pluming itself. I had not noticed its legs at all, and its head, neck, and wings, being constantly moving, I had mistaken for arms, elbows, and towel of a bather, and when it stood stiller its shapely body looked like a peculiar bathing-dress. I floated to within twenty-five rods and watched it at my leisure. Standing on the shallowest part of the bar at that end, it was busily dressing its feathers, passing its bill like a comb down its feathers from base to tip. From its form and color, as well as size, it was singularly distinct. Its great spear-shaped head and bill was very conspicuous, though least so when turned toward me (whom it was eying from time to time). It coils its neck away upon its back or breast as a sailor might a rope, but occasionally stretches itself to its full height, as tall as a man, and looks around and at me. Growing shy, it begins to wade off, until its body

is partly immersed amid the weeds,—potamoge-
tons,—and then it looks more like a goose. The neck
is continually varying in length, as it is doubled up
or stretched out, and the legs also, as it wades in
deeper or shallower water.

Suddenly comes a second, flying low, and
alights on the bar yet nearer to me, almost high and
dry. Then I hear a note from them, perhaps of warning,—a short, coarse, frog-like purring or eructating
sound. You might easily mistake it for a frog. I heard
it half a dozen times. It was not very loud. Anything
but musical. The last proceeds to plume himself,
looking warily at me from time to time, while the
other continues to edge off through the weeds. Now
and then the latter holds its neck as if it were ready
to strike its prey,—stretched forward over the
water,—but I saw no stroke. The arch may be
lengthened or shortened, single or double, but the
great spear-shaped bill and head are ever the same.
A great hammer or pick, prepared to transfix fish,
frog, or bird. At last, the water becoming too deep
for wading, this one takes easily to wing—though
up to his body in water—and flies a few rods to the
shore. It rather flies, then, than swims. It was
evidently scared. These were probably birds of this
season. I saw some distinct ferruginous on the angle
of the wing. There they stood in the midst of the
open river, on this shallow and weedy bar in the
sun, the leisurely sentries, lazily pluming themselves,
as if the day were too long for them. They gave a
new character to the stream. Adjutant they were to
my idea of the river, these two winged men.

You have not seen our weedy river, you do not
know the significance of its weedy bars, until you

have seen the blue heron wading and pluming itself on it. I see that it was made for these shallows, and they for it. Now the heron is gone from the weedy shoal, the scene appears incomplete. Of course, the heron has sounded the depth of the water on every bar of the river that is fordable to it. The water there is not so many feet deep but so many heron's tibí Instead of a foot rule you should use a heron's leg for a measure. If you would know the depth of the water on these few shoalest places of Musketaquid, ask the blue heron that wades and fishes there. In some places a heron can wade across.

How long we may have gazed on a particular scenery and think that we have seen and known it, when, at length, some bird or quadruped comes and takes possession of it before our eyes, and imparts to it a wholly new character. The heron uses these shallows as I cannot. I give them up to him.

December 25, 1859. Standing by the side of the river at Eleazer Davis's Hill,—prepared to pace across it,—I hear a sharp fine *screep* from some bird, which at length I detect amid the button-bushes and willows. The *screep* was a note of recognition meant for me. I saw that it was a novel bird to me. Watching it a long time, with my glass and without it, I at length made out these marks: It was slate-colored above and dirty-white beneath, with a broad and very conspicuous bright-orange crown, which in some lights was *red*-orange, along the middle of the head; this was bounded on each side by a black segment, beneath which was a yellow or whitish line. There was also some yellow and a black spot on the middle of the closed wings, and yellow within the tail-feathers. The ends of the wings and the tail above were dusky, and the tail forked.

It was so very active that I could not get a steady view of it. It kept drifting about behind the stems of the button-bushes, etc., half the time on the ice, and again on the lower twigs, busily looking for its prey, turning its body this way and that with great restlessness, appearing to hide from me behind the stems of the button-bush and the withered coarse grass. When I came nearest it would utter its peculiar *screep*, or screep screep, or even screep screep screep. Yet it was unwilling to leave the spot, and when I cornered it, it hopped back within ten feet of me. However, I could see its brilliant crown, even between the twigs of the button-bush and through the withered grass, when I could detect no other part.

It was evidently the golden-crested wren, which I have not made out before. This little creature was contentedly seeking its food here alone this cold winter day on the shore of our frozen river. If it does not visit us often it is strange that it should choose such a season.

January 4, 1860. In Hosmer's pitch pine wood just north of the bridge, I find myself on the track of a fox — as I take it — that has run about a great deal. Next I come to the tracks of rabbits, see where they have travelled back and forth, making a well-trodden path in the snow; and soon after I see where one has been killed and apparently devoured. There are to be seen only the tracks of what I take to be the fox. The snow is much trampled, or rather flattened by the body of the rabbit. It is somewhat bloody and is covered with flocks of slate-colored and brown fur, an inch and a half long and about as wide, white beneath, and the contents of its paunch or of its entrails are left,—nothing more. Half a dozen rods further, I see where the rabbit has been dropped on the snow again, and some fur is left, and there are the tracks of the fox to the spot and about it. There, or within a rod or two, I notice a considerable furrow in the snow, three or four inches wide and some two rods long, as if one had drawn a stick along, but there is no other mark or track whatever; so I conclude that a partridge, perhaps scared by the fox, had dashed swiftly along so low as to plow the snow. But two or three rods further on one side I see more sign, and lo! there is the remainder of the rabbit,—the whole, indeed, but the tail and the inward or soft parts,—all frozen stiff; but here there is no distinct track of any creature, only a few scratches and marks where

some great bird of prey—a hawk or owl—has struck the snow with its primaries on each side, and one or two holes where it has stood. Now I understand how that long furrow was made, the bird with the rabbit in its talons flying low there, and now I remember that at the first bloody spot I saw some of these quill-marks; and therefore it is certain that the bird had it there, and probably he killed it, and he, perhaps disturbed by the fox, carried it to the second place, and it is certain that he (probably disturbed by the fox again) carried it to the last place, making a furrow on the way.

If it had not been for the snow on the ground I probably should not have noticed any signs that a rabbit had been killed. Or, if I had chanced to see the scattered fur, I should not have known what creature did it, or how recently. But now it is partly certain, partly probable,—or, supposing that the bird could not have taken it from the fox, it is almost all certain,—that an owl or hawk killed a rabbit here last night (the fox-tracks are so fresh), and, when eating it on the snow, was disturbed by a fox, and so flew off with it half a dozen rods, but, being disturbed again by the fox, it flew with it again about as much further, trailing it in the snow for a couple of rods as it flew, and there it finished its meal without being approached. A fox would probably have torn and eaten some of the skin.

When I turned off from the road my expectation was to see some tracks of wild animals in the snow, and, before going a dozen rods, I crossed the track of what I had no doubt was a fox, made apparently the last night,—which had travelled extensively in this pitch pine wood, searching for game.

Then I came to rabbit-tracks, and saw where they had travelled back and forth in the snow in the woods, making a perfectly trodden path, and within a rod of that was a hollow in the snow a foot and a half across, where a rabbit had been killed. There were many tracks of the fox about that place, and I had no doubt then that he had killed that rabbit, and I supposed that some scratches which I saw might have been made by his frisking some part of the rabbit back and forth, shaking it in his mouth. I thought, Perhaps he has carried off to his young, or buried, the rest. But as it turned out, though the circumstantial evidence against the fox was very strong, I was mistaken. I had made him kill the rabbit, and shake and tear the carcass, and eat it all up but the tail (almost); but it seems that he didn't do it at [all], and apparently never got a mouthful of the rabbit. Something, surely, must have disturbed the bird, else why did it twice fly along with the heavy carcass?

The tracks of the bird at the last place were two little round holes side by side, the dry snow having fallen in and concealed the track of its feet.

It was most likely an owl, because it was most likely that the fox would be abroad by night.

The sweet-gale has a few leaves on it yet in some places, partly concealing the pretty catkins.

Again see what the snow reveals. Opposite Dodge's Brook I see on the snow and ice some fragments of frozen-thawed apples under an oak. How came they there? They are apple trees thirty rods off by the road. On the snow under the oak I see two or three tracks of a crow, and the droppings of several that were perched on the tree, and here and there is a perfectly round hole in the snow under the tree. I put down my hand and draw up an apple [out] of each, from beneath the snow. (There are no tracks of squirrels about the oak.) Crows carried these frozen-thawed apples from the apple trees to the oak, and there ate them,—what they did not let fall into the snow or on to the ice.

See that long meandering track where a deer mouse hopped over the soft snow last night, scarcely making any impression. What if you could witness with owl's eyes the revelry of the wood mice some night, frisking about the wood like so many little kangaroos? Here is a palpable evidence that the woods are nightly thronged with little creatures which most have never seen,—such populousness as commonly only the imagination dreams of.

The circumstantial evidence against that fox was very strong, for the deed was done since the snow fell and I saw no other tracks but his at the first places. Any jury would have convicted him, and he would have been hung, if he could have been caught.

January 16, 1860. I see a flock of tree sparrows busily picking something from the surface of the snow amid some bushes. I watch one attentively, and find that it is feeding on the very fine brown chaffy-looking seed of the panicled andromeda. It understands how to get its dinner, to make the plant *give down*, perfectly. It flies up and alights on one of the dense brown panicles of the hard berries, and gives it a vigorous shaking and beating with its claws and bill, sending down a shower of the fine chaffy-looking seed on to the snow beneath. It lies very distinct, though fine almost as dust, on the spotless snow. It then hops down and briskly picks up from the snow what it wants. How very clean and agreeable to the imagination, and withal abundant,

is this kind of food! How delicately they fare! These dry persistant seed-vessels hold their crusts of bread until shaken. The snow is the white tablecloth on which they fall. No anchorite with his water and his crust fares more simply. It shakes down a hundred times as much as it wants at each shrub, and shakes the same or another cluster after each successive snow. How bountifully Nature feeds them! No wonder they come to spend the winter with us, and are at ease with regard to their food. These shrubs ripen an abundant crop of seeds to supply the wants of these immigrants from the far north which annually come to spend the winter with us. How neatly and simply it feeds!

This shrub grows unobserved by most, only known to botanists, and at length matures its hard dry seed-vessels, which, if noticed, are hardly supposed to contain seed. But there is no shrub nor weed which is not known to some bird. Though you may have never noticed it, the tree sparrow comes from the north in the winter straight to this shrub, and confidently shakes its panicle, then feasts on the fine shower of seeds that falls from it.

*A**pril 13, 1860.** P.M. I go up to the Assabet to look at the sweet-gale,which is apparently [?] out at Merrick's shore. It is abundantly out at Pinxter Swamp, and has been some time; so I think I may say that the very first opened April 1st. This may be not only because the season was early and warm, but because the water was so low,—or would that be favorable?

At first I had felt disinclined to make this excursion up the Assabet, but it distinctly occurred to me that, perhaps, if I came against my will, as it were, to look at the sweet-gale as a matter [of]

business, I might discover something else interesting, as when I discovered the sheldrake. As I was paddling past the uppermost hemlocks I saw two peculiar and plump birds near me on the bank there which reminded me of the cow blackbird and of the oriole at first. I saw at once that they were new to me, and guessed that they were crossbills, which was the case,—male and female. The former was dusky-greenish (through a glass), orange, and red, the orange, etc., on head, breast, and rump, the vent white; dark, large bill; the female more of a dusky slate-color, and yellow instead of orange and red. They were very busily eating the seeds of the hemlock, whose cones were strewn on the ground, and they were very fearless, allowing me to approach quite near.

When I returned this way I looked for them again, and at the larger hemlocks heard a peculiar note, *cheep, cheep, cheep, cheep*, in the rhythm of a fish hawk but faster and rather loud, and looking up saw them fly to the north side and alight on the top of a swamp white oak, while I sat in my boat close under the south bank. But immediately they recrossed and went to feeding on the bank within a rod of me. They were very parrot-like both in color (especially the male, greenish and orange, etc.) and in their manner of feeding,—holding the hemlock cones in one claw and rapidly extracting the seeds with their bills, thus trying one cone after another very fast. But they kept their bills a-going [so] that, near as they were, I did not distinguish the cross. I should have looked at them in profile. At last the two hopped within six feet of me, and one within four feet, and they were coming still nearer, as if partly from curiosity, though nibbling the cones all the while, when my chain fell down and rattled loudly,—for the wind shook the boat,—and they flew off a rod. In [Johann Matthaus] Bechstein I read that "it frequents fir and pine woods, but only when there are abundance of the cones." It may be that the abundance of white pine cones last fall had to do with their coming here. The hemlock cones were very abundant too, methinks.

A pril 17, 1860. Looking off on to the river meadow, I noticed, as I thought, a stout stake aslant in the meadow, three or more rods off, sharp at the top and rather light-colored on one side, as is often the case; yet, at the same time, it occurred to me that a stake-driver often resembled a stake very much, but I thought, nevertheless, that there was no doubt about this being a stake. I took out my glass to look for ducks, and my companion, seeing what I had, and asking if it was not a stake-driver, I suffered my glass at last to rest on it, and I was much surprised to find that it was a stake-driver after all. The bird stood in shallow water near a tussock, perfectly still, with its long bill pointed upwards in the same direction with its body and neck, so as perfectly to resemble a stake aslant. If the bill had made an angle with the neck it would have been betrayed at once. Its resource evidently was to rely on its form and color and immobility solely for its concealment. This was its instinct, whether it implies any conscious artifice or not. I watched it for fifteen minutes, and at length it relaxed its muscles and changed its attitude, and I observed a slight motion; and soon after, when I moved toward it, it

flew. It resembled more a piece of a rail than anything else,—more than anything that would have been seen here before the white man came. It is a question whether the bird consciously cooperates in each instance with its Maker, who contrived this concealment. I can never believe that this resemblance is a mere coincidence, not designed to answer this very end—which it does answer so perfectly and usefully.

*A**pril 25, 1860.** Mr. Stewart tells me that he has found a gray squirrel's nest up the Assabet, in a maple tree. I resolve that I too will find it. I do not know within less than a quarter of a mile where to look, nor whether it is in a hollow tree, or in a nest of leaves. I examine the shore first and find where he landed. I then examine the maples in that neighborhood to see what one has been climbed. I soon find one the bark of which has been lately rubbed by the boots of a climber, and, looking up, see a nest. It was a large nest made of maple twigs, with a centre of leaves, lined with finer, about twenty feet from the ground, against the leading stem of a large red maple. I noticed no particular entrance. When I put in my hand from above and felt the young, they uttered a dull croak-like squeak, and one clung fast to my hand when I took it out through the leaves and twigs with which it was covered. It was yet blind, and could not have been many days old, yet it instinctively clung to my hand with its little claws, as if it knew that there was danger of its falling from a height to the ground which it never saw. The idea of clinging was strongly planted in it. There was quite a depth of loose sticks, maple twigs, piled on the top of the nest. No wonder that they became skillful climbers who are born high above the ground and begin their lives in a tree, having first of all to descend to reach the earth. They are cradled in a tree-top, in but a loose basket, in helpless infancy, and there slumber when their mother is away. No wonder that they are never made dizzy by high climbing, that were born in the top of a tree, and learn to cling fast to the tree before their eyes are open.

June 10, 1860. There is much handsome inter-rupted fern in the Painted-Cup Meadow, and near the top of one of the clumps we noticed some-thing like a large cocoon, the color of the rusty cinnamon fern wool. It was a red bat, the New York bat, so called. It hung suspended, head directly downward, with its little sharp claws or hooks caught through one of the divisions at the base of one of the pinnæ, above the fructification. It was a delicate rusty brown in color, very like the wool of the cinnamon fern, with the whiter bare spaces seen through it early in the season. I thought at first glance it was a broad brown cocoon, then that it was the plump body of a monstrous emperor moth. It was rusty or reddish brown, white or hoary within or beneath the tips, with a white apparently triangular spot beneath, about the insertion of the wings. Its wings were very compactly folded up, the principal bones (darker-reddish) lying flat along the under side of its body, and a hook on each meeting its opposite under the chin of the creature. It did not look like fur, but more like the plush of the ripe cat-tail head, though more loose,—all trembling in the wind and with the pulsations of the animal. I broke off the top of the fern and let the bat lie on its back in my hand. I held it and turned it about for ten or fifteen minutes, but it did not awake. Once or twice it opened its eyes a little, and even it raised its head, opened its mouth, but soon drowsily dropped its head and fell asleep again. Its ears were rounded and nearly bare. It was more attentive to sounds than to motions. Finally, by shaking it, and especially by hissing or whistling, I thoroughly awakened it, and it fluttered off twenty or thirty rods to the woods. I cannot but think that its instinct taught it to cling to the interrupted fern, since it might readily be mistaken for a mass of its fruit. Raised its old-haggish head. Unless it showed its head wide awake, it looked like a tender infant.

June 11, 1860. Landing on Tall's Island, I perceive a sour scent from the wilted leaves and scraps of leaves which were blown off yesterday and strew the ground in all woods.

Just within the edge of the wood there, I see a small painted turtle on its back, with its head stretched out as if to turn over. Surprised by the sight, I stopped to investigate the cause. It drew in its head at once, but I noticed that its shell was partially empty. I could see through it from side to side as it lay, its entrails having been extracted through large openings just before the hind legs. The dead leaves were flattened for a foot over, where it had been operated on, and were a little bloody. Its paunch lay on the leaves, and contained much vegetable matter,—old cranberry leaves, etc. Judging by the striæ, it was not more than five or six years old,— or four or five. Its fore parts were quite alive, its hind legs apparently dead, its inwards gone; apparently its spine perfect. The flies had entered it in numbers. What creature could have done this which it would be difficult for a man to do? I thought of a skunk, weazel, mink, but I do not believe that they could have got their snouts into so small a space as that in front of the hind legs between the shells. The hind legs themselves had not been injured nor the shell scratched. I thought it most likely that it was done by some bird of the heron kind which has a long and powerful bill. And probably this accounts for the many dead turtles which I have found and thought died from disease. Such is Nature, who gave one creature a taste or yearning for another's entrails as its favorite tidbit!! I thought the more of a bird, for, just as we were shoving away from this isle, I heard a sound just like a small dog barking hoarsely, and, looking up, saw it was made by a bittern (*Ardea minor*), a pair of which were flapping over the meadows and probably had a nest in some tussock thereabouts. No wonder the turtle is wary, for, notwithstanding its horny shell, when it comes forth to lay its eggs it runs the risk of having its entrails plucked out. That is the reason that the box turtle, which lives on the land, is made to shut itself up entirely within the shell, and I suspect that the mud tortoise only comes forth by night. What need the turtle has of some horny shield over those tender parts and avenues to its entrails! I saw several of these painted turtles dead on the bottom.

*S*eptember 27, 1860. A.M. Sawing up my raft by river. River about thirty-five inches above summer level, and goes no higher this time.

Monroe's tame ducks sail along and feed close to me as I am working there. Looking up, I see a little dipper, about one half their size, in the middle of the river, evidently attracted by these tame

ducks, as to a place of security. I sit down and watch it. The tame ducks have paddled four or five rods downstream along the shore. They soon detect the dipper three or four rods off, and betray alarm by a tittering note, especially when it dives, as it does continually. At last, when it is two or three rods off and approaching them by diving, they all rush to the shore and come out on it in their fear, but the dipper shows itself close to the shore, and when they enter the water again joins them within two feet, still diving from time to time and threatening to come up in their midst. They return upstream, more or less alarmed, and pursued in this wise by the dipper, who does not know what to make of their fears, and soon the dipper is thus tolled along to within twenty feet of where I sit, and I can watch at my leisure. It has a dark bill and considerable white on the sides of the head or neck, with black between it, no tufts, and no observable white back or tail. When at last disturbed by me, it suddenly sinks low (all its body) in the water without diving. Thus it can float at various heights. (So on the 30th I saw one suddenly dash along the surface from the meadow ten rods before me to the middle of the river, and then dive, and though I watched fifteen minutes and examined the tufts of grass, I could see no more of it.)

February 21, 1861. This plucking and stripping a pine cone is a business which he [a squirrel] and his family understand perfectly. That is their *forte*. I doubt if you could suggest any improvement. After ages of experiment their instinct has settled on the same method that our reason would finally, if we had to open a pine cone with our teeth; and they were thus accomplished before our race knew that a pine cone contained any seed.

He does not prick his fingers, nor pitch his whiskers, nor gnaw the solid core any more than is necessary. Having sheared off the twigs and needles that may be in his way,—for like a skillful woodchopper he first secures room and verge enough,—he neatly cuts off the stout stem of the cone with a few strokes of his chisels, and it is his. To be sure, he may let it fall to the ground and look down at it for a moment curiously, as if it were not his; but he is taking note where it lies and adding it to a heap of a hundred more like it in his mind, and it now is only so much the more his for his seeming carelessness. And, when the hour comes to open it, observe how he proceeds. He holds it in his hands,—a solid embossed cone, so hard it almost rings at the touch of his teeth. He pauses for a moment perhaps,—but not because he does not know how to begin,—he only listens to hear what is in the wind, not being in a hurry. He knows better than to try to cut off the tip and work his way downward against a *chevaux-de-frise* of advanced scales and prickles, or to gnaw into the side for three quarters of an inch in the face of many armed shields. But he does not have to think of what he knows, having heard the last æolian rumor. If there ever was an age of the world when the squirrels opened their cones wrong end foremost, it was not the golden age at any rate. He whirls the cone bottom upward in a twinkling, where the scales are smallest and the prickles slight or none and the short stem is cut so close as not to be in his way, and then he proceeds to cut through the thin and tender bases of the scales, and each stroke tells, laying bare at once a couple of seeds. And then he strips it as easily as if its scales were chaff, and so rapidly, twirling it as he advances, that you cannot tell how he does it till you drive him off and inspect his unfinished work.